Book Design
SIMPLE & PROFESSIONAL

HALF TITLE PAGE | RIGHT-HAND PAGE
NO FOOTER OR HEADER | NO PAGE NUMBER | OPTIONAL

BLANK PAGE FOLLOWS IF USING HALF TITLE PAGE
NO FOOTER OR HEADER | NO PAGE NUMBER | OPTIONAL

Book Design

SIMPLE & PROFESSIONAL

For self-publishers and
graphic artists using
Adobe® InDesign®

Nancy Starkman

Author BOOK STUDIO
Bellevue, Washington

Book Design: Simple & Professional | Nancy Starkman

Author Book Studio
6514 153rd Ave SE
Bellevue, WA 98006
425.603.1777

PUBLISHER
Author Book Studio
a division of Star Print Brokers, Inc.

INTERIOR & COVER DESIGN
Nancy Starkman

WEBSITE
AuthorBookStudio.com

EMAIL
info@authorbookstudio.com

LIBRARY OF CONGRESS CONTROL NUMBER
2020925686

ISBN
978-0-578-24407-5

FIRST PRINTING
February 2021
Printed in South Korea

Publisher's Cataloging-in-Publication data

Names: Starkman, Nancy, author.

Title: Book design : simple & professional, for self-publishers and graphic artists using Adobe® InDesign® / Nancy Starkman.

Description: Includes index. | Bellevue, WA: Author Book Studio, 2021.

Identifiers: LCCN: 2020925686 | ISBN: 978-0-578-24407-5

Subjects: LCSH Adobe InDesign (Electronic resource) – Handbooks, manuals, etc. | Book design – Handbooks, manuals, etc. | Graphic design (Typography) | Self-publishing – Handbooks, manuals, etc. | Layout (Printing) | BISAC DESIGN / Book | DESIGN / Graphic Arts / General | DESIGN / Graphic Arts / Typography | COMPUTERS / Design, Graphics & Media / Graphics Tools

Classification: LCC Z246 .S73 2021 | DDC 686.2/252--dc23

Copyright © 2021 by Nancy Starkman. All rights reserved. This book may not be reproduced or utilized in any form or by any means, electronic or mechanical, including photography, recording, or by any information storage and retrieval system, without permission in writing from the author. All photographs and images are used with permission.

The information in this book is distributed on an "as is" basis, without warranty. While every precaution has been taken in the preparation of this book, neither the author, Author Book Studio, nor Star Print Brokers, Inc. shall have any liability to any person or entity with respect to any liability, loss, or damage caused or alleged to be caused directly or indirectly by the instructions contained in this book or by the computer software or hardware products described herein.

BOOK DESIGN: SIMPLE & PROFESSIONAL IS NOT AUTHORIZED, ENDORSED OR SPONSORED BY ADOBE, PUBLISHER OF Adobe InDesign, Adobe Photoshop, Adobe Acrobat, Adobe Illustrator, and Adobe Fonts. Adobe, InDesign, Photoshop, Acrobat, Illustrator, Adobe Camera Raw, Adobbe Flash Player, and Adobe Fonts are registered trademarks or trademarks of Adobe Inc., which is incorporated in the United States and other countries. Microsoft, Windows, Word and Excel are registered trademarks of Microsoft Corporation. Pantone, Pantone Matching System, Pantone Color Bridge, PMS, Pantone Colors, Pantone Names, numbers, formulas, or trademarks or copyrights of Pantone LLC.

Book Design: Simple & Professional is an independent book and has not been authorized, sponsored, or otherwise approved by Apple Inc. Apple®, Mac®, and Macintosh® are trademarks of Apple, Inc. Google Fonts, Google Search, Google AdWords are registered trademarks of Google LLC. Wire-O® is a registered trademark of James Burn International.

Book Design: Simply & Professional has no affiliation with or endorsement by the WordPress Foundation or the WordPress open source project. The trademark symbol will be used once for each trademarked software hardware, product, or service. There is no intention or infringement of the trademarks. None of the aforementioned trademarks or their owners authorize, endorse, or sponsor Book Design: Simple & Professional. All trademarks are products of their respective owners.

Books may be available for bulk sale.

This book is printed on acid-free paper.

To writers who dream of becoming published authors

For creatives who dream of designing books

May all your dreams come true

*"The way we're running the company,
the product design, the advertising,
it all comes down to this:
Let's make it simple. Really simple."*

—STEVE JOBS

CONTENTS

Preface   *xi*

   PART ONE

CHAPTER 1
DESIGN FUNDAMENTALS   1

Basic principles overview	3
Typography	8
Color	13
Layout	14
Tips for better book design	15

CHAPTER 2
PLANNING A BOOK   33

Preferences for Adobe InDesign	34
Standard book sizes	35
Paper stock	38
Choosing typefaces	39
Selecting a color scheme	43
Working with color in text	45
Page margins	48
Book page layouts	50
Cover considerations	54
Manuscript and captions	57
Collecting photos and images	59
Resolution for book printing	60
Actual and effective resolution	63
Author and designer responsibilities	64

CHAPTER 3
BOOK STRUCTURE   67

Divisions in a book	67
Front matter	69
Text or body matter	70
Back matter	70

PART TWO

CHAPTER 4
GETTING STARTED — 73

    The Grid System and the Big Picture — 75
    Creating a grid in InDesign — 77
    White space — 80
    InDesign files needed by book binding — 82
    Coffee table books — 83
    Cookbooks — 83
    Novels — 85
    Photography and art books — 85
    Picture books — 86
    Board books — 89
    Reference books — 89

CHAPTER 5   QUICK START
INTERIOR PAGES — 91

    Book and page documents *SET-UP* — 92
    Page masters and numbering *SET-UP* — 95
    Paragraph Style *SET-UP* — 96
    Character Style *SET-UP* — 97
    Headers and footers *SET-UP* — 98
    Placing the manuscript — 100
    Synchronizing documents in a book — 100

CHAPTER 6   QUICK START
COVER DESIGN & BINDING — 103

    Book cover design — 103
    ISBN and barcode — 104
    Retail price — 105
    Spine width and printer templates — 106
    Soft cover InDesign file *SET-UP* — 107
    Hardcover with printed cover wrap *SET-UP* — 108
    Hardcover with cover wrap material *SET-UP* — 109
    Wire-O bindings *SET-UP* — 111
    Standard dust jacket *SET-UP* — 112

PART TWO CONTINUED

CHAPTER 7
EXTRAS FOR BOOKS 115

    Printed endpapers *SET-UP*   115
    Duotones *SET-UP*   118
    Slip cases   120
    Bumper boxes   121
    Head and tail bands   122
    Ribbon markers   123
    Lamination   123
    Soft cover French flaps *SET-UP*   124
    French fold dust jacket *SET-UP*   125
    Vellum tip-in sheet   126
    Belly band   126
    Tip-on cover sticker *SET-UP*   127
    Spot varnish *SET-UP*   128
    Foil emboss *SET-UP*   130
    Book sleeve   131
    Journal with elastic band   132
    Hardcover endpaper pockets   133

PART THREE

CHAPTER 8
PRINTING ON PRESS 135

    Authentic book printing and binding   137
    Traditional binding vs. print-on-demand   140
    Color printing   141
    Why is the color off?   144
    Hardcover spines and binding   147
    Soft cover spines and binding   149
    Create the PDF to print on press   152
    Uploading or sending files   153

PART FOUR

CHAPTER 9
SELLING & MARKETING — 155

The package deals	157
Branding considerations	159
Pricing strategy	161
Amazon	162
Fulfillment	163
Distribution	164
Social media	166
Marketing	168

CHAPTER 10
BUILD A WEBSITE — 171

Website sitebuilders	171
Established websites	172
WordPress	174
Search Engine Optimization (SEO)	177
Email list and newsletters	179

Glossary	*183*
Resources	*191*
Fractional equivalents: pounds / points / GSM	*192*
Paper equivalents: Asia & Europe vs. USA	*193*
Comparable Pounds to GSM paper weight	*194*
Chart for other paper needs	*194*
Index	*195*

PREFACE

Few schools teach book design

This book is about how to design a book. It is less about how to use Adobe® InDesign®. However, the chapters include step-by-step Adobe InDesign instructions for different book design set-ups. Illustrations give a clearer explanation when words are not enough.

While graphic artists may get a formal design education, few schools will teach book design specifically. More and more graphic artists are focused on web design web and not design for books printing on press.

A book designer most often learns their craft from personal experience and the act of designing a book. The opportunity for a graphic artist to design a book does not happen as often as working on other types of projects. Many do not get the full book design experience.

Self-publishers have different motives to learn book design. They may want to design their book to have full control over its design and layout, or just save money on design fees. *Book Design: Simple & Professional* fills the gap. There are many books and sources from which to learn Adobe InDesign. Learn book design here; that is to properly structure and design professional looking books.

When there is a section that requires an InDesign set-up, instructions are provided. It is assumed that the reader is somewhat proficient in InDesign. Visit Adobe InDesign Help if necessary. Go to the menu in InDesign and select Help > InDesign Help . . .

Keep book design simple. Those who have some experience may want to go directly to the book and cover design steps. They are in Chapter 5, *Interior Text Design* and Chapter 6, *Cover Design & Binding*. Both chapters have dark gray borders that provide a quick visual reference. French flaps are added to the front and back book covers to save your place(s) in the book.

Light gray type is found on the bottom of some pages in front matter and back matter. It provides extra guidance for each of these pages. This is in addition to the chart that *The Chicago Manual of Style* was kind enough to give their permission to use. See Chapter 3, *Book Structure*, page 68.

If you are a novice, grounding yourself thoroughly in the basics is advisable. An author asked the following question which ultimately lead to the design of this book:

> *Q: I am printing a series of coffee table books and need someone to guide me through the process of creating the book. I have much of the content already. Can we set up a time to speak?*

> A: We do not provide individual instruction; however, you may call during normal business hours, and we would be happy to have a brief discussion. First, collect images in some organized way. Creating an art folder or chapter folders. Write the manuscript and captions in Microsoft Word. Indicate where the images will go in the manuscript. The book should be designed using Adobe InDesign.

Sounds simple, but there is a lot more to book design. I am happy to have conversations about book design. Some self-publishers expect a short answer, condensing decades of knowledge and experience into brief answers about how to design their specific book. Time does not allow for personal instruction. I love to help self-publishers and graphic artists. This simple and professional book offers guidance, expertise, and useful book design tips.

There are graphic artists who do an amazing job on their first book. We are wowed when see their design! However, many get lost in the weeds when book design is new to them. A self-publisher naturally thinks that graphic artists design books. Frequently, they have never designed a book, but may have a wonderful portfolio of other work. Some may have limited or no experience in book design. They may just be a desktop publisher . . . for now.

The desktop publisher is different. They have a computer and maybe InDesign. Perhaps they have some experience in graphic design. A novel can be designed in Microsoft® Word®. A coffee table book, children's book, photography book, or cookbook is another story. *InDesign is the standard.*

Vast numbers of books were written over the centuries about typography. Self-publishers who want to design their book, may dive in without understanding the basic principles of typography, page layout, and color reproduction. They need to know about book printing on press, image resolution, and the variations of different types of book bindings. Since few schools teach book design, the focus of this book is to make the new book designer's job easier and faster.

Book designers charge more because they know more. Desktop publishers charge less because they have less knowledge and may just want the prestige of a book project for which they are ill-prepared. *It will show.*

Well-designed books command a higher retail price. Self-publishers often do not realize that better design brings more book sales. Designing a beautiful or striking book is one of the most important factors in marketing. Authors cannot charge top dollar for books with poor design. They may have to charge less.

I founded Star Print Brokers Inc. in 1999 with my husband, Edward Starkman. We provide high-quality book printing at a reasonable unit cost. Print-on-demand is not a service we offer, nor is printing in China. The quality is not up to our standards.

Extra options can be added and are often not found anywhere else. Detailed in this book are options and services differences. Star Print Brokers is a high-quality alternative to other vendors. Time and money are wasted if a book is designed with unavailable options. It is up to the author to finalize book specifications by consulting with their vendor.

Book Design: Simple & Professional is a guide to learn more, streamline the design process, and create a better book design. Self-publishers can charge more for books with a professional looking design. When a graphic designer learns more about book design, they can charge more for their services.

Nancy Östling Starkman
February 2021

PART ONE

Plan

- Basic principles overview
- Typography
- Color
- Layout
- Tips for better book design

DESIGN FUNDAMENTALS
Basics for Books

SELF-PUBLISHERS NEED TO UNDERSTAND THE BASICS of design and layout. Set the document page size and first chapter or front matter in Adobe® InDesign®. This chapter covers design fundamentals.

 QUICK TIPS

- Writing the manuscript in Microsoft® Word® is preferable.
- Have someone else proofread the manuscript and captions.
- Images must be 300 ppi *or larger*, **and** at the approximate size they will be when printed in the book, *or larger*.
- Create an "original" folder for all images. Duplicate the folder. Use the duplicate folder for the book. Rename each to identify placement or organize images in chapter folders.
- Have the manuscript and images in hand before beginning the design. Do not start without *everything*.
- Most designers have a passion for typography. There are basic principles to understand. The goal is a professional book design.
- Select typography and basic page layout. Work in one chapter until choices are final.

Basic principles overview

Search for "principles of design" in a search engine. According to various sources, there are anywhere from four to eleven principles of design. Views differ on page construction and typography.

- Typography, page layout, and color form the foundation of good design.
- The design depends on the audience, subject matter, and style.
- Page layout including the elements of alignment, balance, contrast, hierarchy, repetition, and white space are all part of a cohesive design.

Photo by Fabrice Villard on Unsplash

Foundation

The following general overview of subjects lays the foundation upon which book design and page layout are built.

Understanding these subjects elevates the book designer's skills and enhances their ability to turn out well-designed books. Not only does the understanding of fundamentals translate to more pride in one's work, but it also means that the designer can charge more for better design capabilities.

LAYOUT

Well-designed books capture the reader's attention. There is an infinite number of ways to layout a book. Plan the layout early in the design process, as one would create an itinerary for a trip. Start with the structure of the book, considering the overall feel, typeface, and plan where the images are to be placed.

Design one basic page first. Modify it or create versions of the basic page for specific needs.

TYPOGRAPHY

Graphic designers often use *contrast* as a principle in typography. However, one can certainly use just one font for all text and headlines. Simply expand the tracking of the body text font for headlines and change them to uppercase. While acceptable, this provides little contrast. But, that is the point. The use of contrast is the designer's decision.

A book design utilizing typography alone can be very striking. Sometimes less really is more. Train your eye by studying a variety of well-designed books. See page 8 in this chapter for more on typography.

COLOR

The color palette is an exciting and sometimes frustrating subject when designing a book. Know how to choose color, and how to use the InDesign Swatches palette.

The understanding of color reproduction on press is necessary to know what to expect on the printed page. That means learning about color on press when printing in process color or solid, spot inks. RGB will only sometimes match the CMYK screen build. Know what is possible, so there are no surprises. See Chapter 8, *Printing on Press*, page 141 for more on color.

Design

The book's potential audience, its subject matter, and overall style are three major factors in determining the design of a book. Studying audience interests and demographics, the book's subject matter, and examining the proposed style of a book will lead a designer to decisions that determine the final design.

AUDIENCE

Who will buy the book? How and where will it be sold? It is helpful to write a paragraph about the book buyer to determine demographics and interests.

Define the demographic which may include age, gender, marital status, income, education, employment, interests, and hobbies. What categories will the book be listed in on Amazon®? Who will the target market be on Facebook®? This exercise will help with the Amazon author page, social media, and keyword and keyword phrase choices for better SEO.

SUBJECT MATTER

Always consider the content and subject matter of a book to be designed. Many self-publishers are writing books that fit into the following short list of book types.

We will go over the set-ups for each type: coffee table books, cookbooks, novels, photography and art books, picture books, board books, reference books. There are many other types of books and subjects that fall into a book type on the short list. See Chapter 4, *Getting Started, starting on page 83* for features of these different book types.

STYLE

A coffee table book on flower arranging is in a completely different style than an automotive reference manual. The layout, typography, and color scheme play into the book design style. Feel free to use luscious photography, stylized headlines, and create interesting graphics.

Style can mean elegance, grunge, romance, or a myriad of possibilities. Most of us appreciate a beautiful book or a well-thought out reference guide. An example might be a reference book. But if your audience does not care if a book is beautiful, then give them organized, functional design with easy to read content. Follow basic design principles to achieve a professional look, no matter the book style.

Page layout

A book designer uses information to make layout decisions. There are certain foundation concepts that make sense to follow. The rest is guidance that is picked up from a multitude of information gathered over the years.

A designer may tend to over design. Walk away from the book and return to it the next day. Then remove the unnecessary elements. If stalled in the design process, go back to the necessary foundation subjects that inspires.

It should be understood to never copy or plagiarize, but design is your own creation. Putting a new twist on a retro style becomes a new design. Blend your own ideas into the process while maintaining structure in the page and with the typography and essential use of white space.

ALIGNMENT

A clean design is managed by using alignment. Graphic elements as well as type should be aligned using a grid. A grid may or may not be in place underlying the type. But aligning type creates a unified look. See the front cover of this book as an example of type that is aligned. Also see Chaper 4, *Getting Started*, page 75, for more about grids.

BALANCE

Balance is the arrangement graphic elements, type, color, and white space. Distribute graphic elements symmetrically or asymmetrically.

Symmetrical balance is used on one side of the design. Asymmetrical balance is adding elements differently, but they still look balanced. A grid is helpful. Establish styles and adhere to them throughout the book.

HIERARCHY

The most important message needs to be the dominant element on the page. What do you want the reader to see first? Establish styles for headlines and subheads. Getting creative, it could also mean starting a chapter with a large colorful quote in script.

All books should use a headline larger than the text, perhaps in bold or all uppercase letters. Then create a slightly smaller subhead, possibly in a semi-bold or italic font. A third subhead may be smaller, but still serves as a headline for a paragraph. Three headlines or subheads is all you need. If adding any more subheads, evaluate whether it is really needed. If you have a tendency to over design, try to simplify design elements.

CONTRAST

Imagine large type overlaying a full bleed photograph. That is contrast. Small type is best for captions, but not for headlines unless making a special design statement.

Another way to add contrast is an exceptionally large headline or quote that contrasts in size against smaller body text.

REPETITION

Once the book's typefaces, paragraph and headline styles, and color are established, the rule of repetition should be followed. Use the same logo or icons, same color, same typography, and the same feel to create the brand.

Branding is not just a logo or stylized book title. It is the repetition in the overall book style and all materials used to market a book, service, product, or company. Branding includes the repetition of chosen elements on the website, print materials, landing pages, memes, social media, and advertisements. Establish the brand and repeat the elements everywhere. Repetition helps to establish or support the brand and the book design.

Be careful that many new styles are not created when a set of basic styles will provide a unified look. Simplicity is a characteristic of all well-designed books and it can be accomplished by repeating the same elements instead of constantly creating new bits of design.

WHITE SPACE

Perhaps one of the most overlooked and abused aspects of good design is the use, or rather non-use, of white space.

Good use of white space draws the reader's attention to the elements on the page, whether they are well-formed paragraphs or an image. Avoid the temptation to fill up every little bit of white space. Narrow page margins with oversized type could make the reader uncomfortable.

A page with one small element and mostly white will attract more attention than a crowded page of text with skimpy margins. White space is dramatic! Do not be afraid to use it.

Typography

Book designers should be passionate about typography. It means everything to strong page design. A designer with a foundation in the history of type, typefaces, font construction, and various type foundries is invaluable.

Make typography a priority in book design. A reliable, often classic typeface provides a solid basis for body text. A hierarchy is used in typography when selecting typefaces and fonts for headlines, subheads, captions, quotes, and more. Authors need to send the right message to readers. Typography can be that strong communicator. Good use of typography can draw the reader to the message and hold their attention. Poor typography can make the designer and the book look amateurish.

START WITH A HIGH-QUALITY TYPEFACE

Using classic "pro" typefaces is the basis for typography that is timeless. Limit typefaces to one or two families. They need to be paired correctly. A third font can be used if you have a stylized use in mind. An example might be setting the title of a recipe in script—not in uppercase—or a handwriting font. Consider typeface with useful glyphs.

Beautiful or poor typography can make or break a book when it comes to sales. There are thousands of available typefaces today. Do not get lost in all the choices. Limit choices for a simple and professional book design.

Type classification

There are different typeface classifications. Adobe Fonts uses Sans Serif, Serif, Slab Serif, Script, Blackletter, Mono, Hand, and Decorative. Google Fonts uses Serif, Sans Serif, Display, Handwriting, and Monospace. Classification seems to be a matter of choice; however, serif and sans serif always top the list.

Although typeface selections for book design and website design may be chosen from both Adobe Fonts and Google Fonts, we prefer Adobe Fonts for professional book design. There are many fine type foundries that may or may not have typefaces listed on Adobe Fonts. Designers and self-publishers should explore them as well.

The examples on the next page show *serif* and *sans serif* letters. **Serif** type on the left in the illustration has feet, or a beak or the arms that are circled. "Sans" simply means "without." In this case, without feet. The example on the right in the same illustration is **sans serif**.

Serif (Minion Pro)

Sans Serif (Myriad Pro)

Typeface

An entire alphabet with letters, numbers, punctuation, and some having additional glyphs is termed a **typeface**. A well-known typeface is Helvetica.

> Helvetica

Typeface family

A range of fonts all based on the same typeface is a **typeface family**. Examples of a family include Helvetica and other variations. There are many more examples of Helvetica variations to include in a typeface family.

> Helvetica, Helvetica Narrow, Helvetica Neue LT Std.

Fonts

The different styles included in a typeface are called **fonts**. Each example listed below is a font.

> Helvetica Regular
> *Helvetica Oblique*
> **Helvetica Bold**
> ***Helvetica Bold Oblique***
>
> Helvetica Narrow Regular
> *Helvetica Narrow Oblique*
> **Helvetica Narrow Bold**
> ***Helvetica Narrow Bold Oblique***
> Helvetica Neue LT Std Roman

> Helvetica Neue LT Std Roman
> *Helvetica Neue LT Std Italic*
> **Helvetica Neue LT Std Bold**
> ***Helvetica Neue LT Std Bold Italic***
>
> *Helvetica Neue LT Std Italic*
> **Helvetica Neue LT Std Bold**
> ***Helvetica Neue LT Std Bold Italic***

Superfamilies

Typefaces that can be grouped because they share the same basic style are called **superfamilies**. Helvetica and Helvetica Narrow qualify as a superfamily. So do typefaces that have both serif and sans serif fonts, like Freight for example.

CHAPTER ONE | DESIGN FUNDAMENTALS

FreightSans Pro

FreightText Pro

FreightNeo Pro

Each of these typeface families contains 24 fonts. A typical way to use the fonts is for headlines and body text, like using two of the following:

FreightSans Pro Bold	headline
FreightText Pro Black	headline
FreightText Pro Book	body text
FreightNeo Pro Book	body text

Open Type Variable Typefaces

VARIABLE FONTS

Adobe Fonts introduced Variable fonts in June 2020. They are Open Typefaces, but they are also "Variable." The fonts are in a new, customizable format. The purpose is to have more variety from a single font than you can have from an entire font family. To access Variable fonts activated with Adobe Fonts, go to (Ctrl + T) > Font Family drop down.

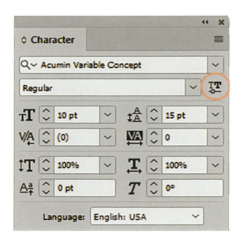

We are using Acumin Pro Variable Concept in this example. When viewing the list of typefaces on the computer, there are symbols for Open fonts or True Type fonts. The new symbol for a variable font is the "O" with "VAR" in smaller letters covering the "O."

See the illustration to the left and notice the circled icon. Click to the see the pull-down menu. This is where you can adjust the weight, width, and slant. Selection is made by moving the sliders.

I still prefer utilizing typefaces as the designer originally designed them. Skill goes into designing character shapes. It seems that some Variable Fonts skew the characters if not adjusted proportionally.

10   BOOK DESIGN: SIMPLE & PROFESSIONAL

ADJUSTING NON-VARIABLE TYPEFACES

It is not advisable to artificially condense or expand the actual characters in non-variable typefaces. However, *kerning*, meaning adding or reducing space between letters, is common.

Top typeface designers and foundries work extremely hard to get each character in a typeface exactly right. It is a lot of work and these professional typefaces may be pricey. But these typeface families are especially worth the extra cost. Not only is each unique, but they are well-built.

Most often, select typefaces have beautiful or interesting glyphs to use. While variable fonts open new possibilities, one rule remains the same. Too many font variations clutter the design. Limit choices and use Paragraph Styles and Character Styles to keep the design simple.

Typeface superfamilies are safe to use. Condensed versions of a typeface may be selected, but not all typefaces have condensed fonts. Design the paragraph text, headlines, and subheads early. Work with them in a few pages or samples until they suit your design.

It is interesting to experiment with typefaces by one-off designers, but I am reluctant to do so until they are more experienced. I prefer using typefaces from Adobe Fonts or well-known foundries.

Designing type may pique your interest. Typeface design takes knowledge, expertise, and time. A self-publisher does not need to design a typeface for use in one book when there is a multitude of options available.

About glyphs

A glyph is the design of a character. There may be several different glyphs for each character in a typeface. Many professional typefaces have a range of unexpected and very creative glyphs—which may include borders, border corner elements, and more.

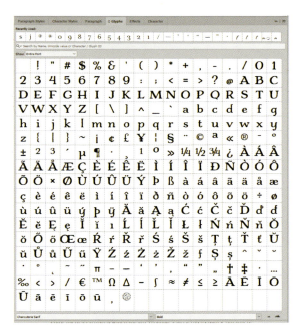

Glyphs in Charcuterie Serif Bold.

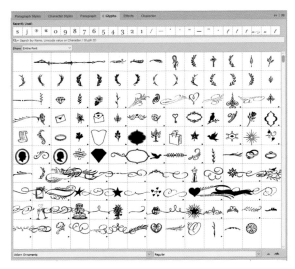

Glyphs in Adorn Ornaments Regular.

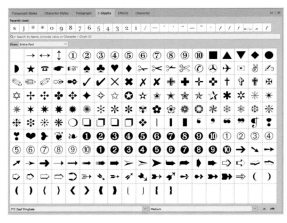

ITC Zapf Dingbats Medium

When buying or selecting typefaces for use in book design, check the character map to see all the available glyphs.

There may be particular fractions needed for cookbook recipes, icons, symbols, numbers, scientific inferiors, or glyphs for math symbols.

Look at different pro typefaces as they might save book design time as well as add interest. Be careful not to over design as too many elements make the design look cluttered.

Zapf Dingbats

A **dingbat** is a glyph character in Zapf Dingbats which is a typeface designed by Hermann Zapf in 1978. It has been used for years as a staple for graphic designers. However, a wide variety of dingbats is seen in many other typefaces.

More dingbats are available in other typefaces, icons, and graphics. Whether using Zapf Dingbats or not, it is a great typeface to own and may prove useful.

Explore other dingbat typefaces for a variety of uses.

Color

Much of achieving great color on press depends on how the files are prepared, the use of process or spot color, and understanding CMYK and RGB color modes.

While one can use primary, secondary, and tertiary colors on the color wheel, problems may arise when trying to replicate those colors on press. Colors used on a monitor in RGB may not replicate well.

I bought a book years ago that was specifically for color schemes. It provided the CMYK screen builds for printing, and RGB and HTML values for online.

Most of the CMYK and RGB combinations did not match. Also, the publisher did not have a good printer. Hardly anything matched as I tried to replicate color in the book to what I saw on my monitor. The color did not match the Pantone Color Bridge®. Although my monitor was not calibrated, the press proofs for the books that I designed matched the monitor perfectly.

Our business is built not only on our expertise, but also the use of our cadre of excellent printers. Having worked in color houses years ago, experience taught me two important things to keep in mind. Before assigning blame for bad color reproduction, understand these fundamentals:

CMYK PROCESS AND SPOT EQUIVALENTS

CMYK screen builds and solid spot PMS inks match only about half the time. See the Pantone Color Bridge for quick verification. It is an essential tool every book designer should use.

PRINTING ON PRESS TO MATCH RGB

Replicating RGB on press can be difficult or often impossible. That is because printing on press always prints ink in CMYK, which is process color.

The inks are Cyan, Magenta, Yellow, and blacK. These four inks combine to create process color. Process has a narrower array of color than RGB which is Red, Green, Blue. RGB is used on screens for computer monitors, iPads, and iPhones, and other digital devices.

See more about color in Chapter 8 *Printing on Press*, page 141.

Layout

Book sizes are discussed in subsequent chapters. However, this chapter covers fundamentals for non-designers. Once the page size is determined, place the manuscript, and begin the book design process. Organize the text, images, and graphic elements to create an appealing book design.

Do not be intimidated by changes. It is a nearly foregone conclusion that whatever you start with in book design will change, several times. Documents can be synchronized so that changes can be reflected in all chapters. See book synchronization in Chapter 5, *Interior Pages* on page 100.

Start with one basic master page

Create a one page design to expand later into different versions. Choose these elements:

- Typeface(s)
- Types sizes and line spacing for headlines, subheads, text, and captions
- Page margins
- Page number style and footer or header style
- Color(s) or color scheme
- Paragraph styles
- Character styles
- Additional master pages

Add page versions

Consider the function of a book for master pages. A novel has one column of text on each page. A reference book may have two or more columns.

An art or photography book may have several complimentary master pages. For instance, the body text on a three-column page may span two columns with an adjacent image. The text in the third column might be the space for a caption or side bar. Keep the gutter width the same for a unified design. Establish rules for your design and adhere to them.

There is a master page for each chapter in this book to accommodate chapter names and make chapters more manageable.

See Chapter 5, *Interior Pages* on page 91.

See Chapter 6, *Cover Design & Binding* on page 103.

Tips for better book design

This section includes some of the most common ways to improve the design of a book. They are in no particular order. Start by choosing typefaces with a range of weights. Create a hierarchy in headlines and subheadlines.

Create Paragraph Styles and Character Styles

PARAGRAPH STYLES

When designing Paragraph Styles, create and name the style, and then apply the style's attributes. A helpful hint is to keep some styles in a group folder, like "Front Matter" for example.

When designing headlines, it is helpful to use placeholder text below headers to see how they look. Create a hierarchy of headline styles. H1, h2, h3, and h4 may be alternative names.

Uppercase and lowercase letters are easier to read. When using all uppercase letters, be deliberate but do not overdo the use of uppercase.

Headline (h1):	**Headline**
Subhead (h2):	***Subhead***
Sub-subhead (h3):	**SUB-SUBHEAD**
Sub-sub-subhead (h4):	***Sub-sub-subhead***

A novel uses limited text and headline styles. When designing a cookbook or a stylistic coffee table book, more styles may be included. See Paragraph styles in Chapter 5 *Interior Pages* on pages 96.

CHARACTER STYLES

Character Styles are handy when Paragraph Styles are too much. Character Styles have a more limited role. Words that are to be **bold** or *italics* throughout can be set up. See Character Styles in Chapter 5 *Interior Pages* on pages 97.

Body text with emphasis

If using a bold font for emphasis in regular text, make it **two font steps bolder** than the text font. Type a paragraph to view the weights. The contrast depends on the typeface used as well as the font weight. See the first example on the next page with a bolder font. The difference is barely noticeable. The second example is much more effective.

Example 1: Freight Text Pro: Book & Medium (1-step difference):

A paragraph with emphasis when a sentence or a word has a one-step darker font: Ibus ut labo. Isi ut preictae rest maiorep taspici litatur?

Emperum quibus aut es nem haribus et maximen turersp errorrum quodio voloriat quam quaepuditiam et archil.

Example 2: Freight Text Pro: Book & Black (2-step difference):

A paragraph with more emphasis when a sentence or a word has a two-step darker font: **Ibus ut labo. Isi ut preictae rest maiorep taspici litatur?**

Emperum quibus aut es nem haribus et **maximen** turersp errorrum quodio voloriat quam quaepuditiam et archil.

The choice can also be a lighter text weight with a darker emphasis font. Font names vary among typefaces.

LIGHT & DARK FONTS:

Light plus **Medium fonts**
Book plus **Semibold fonts**
Medium plus **Bold fonts**
Semibold plus **Black fonts**

FREIGHTTEXT PRO FONTS:

FreightText Pro Light
FreightText Pro Book
FreightText Pro Medium
FreightText Pro Semibold
FreightText Pro Bold
FreightText Pro Black

Two typeface families

One typeface is for headlines and another for body text, but try to use no more than two typeface families. If necessary, a third typeface might be used, like a script or specialty font for use in cookbooks or chapter headlines.

Typefaces need to be paired correctly. Superfamilies are great for this purpose. We use Mr Eaves and another typeface, Mrs Eaves, for text. One way to pair fonts is to look for the same x-height or same shape characters in both serif and sans serif typefaces.

Make type size reader friendly

The readable text size should be between 10- and 12-point, but typefaces can vary in size because of the shape of the letters. They vary too, in their weight, or the thickness of the characters. The height of the lowercase letters can be different among typefaces.

A 12-point font can be too large in some typefaces, especially those with a larger x-height. That is the height of lowercase letters without ascenders. The only constant is the height of the uppercase letters.

Set some sample text blocks of the body copy to see what the typeface looks like in various sizes. It must be readable. The samples should also test line spacing (leading) and line length.

Reader friendly type size and leading examples:

Correct

Century Gothic Regular
11 pt type, 16 pt leading (11/16)
Listio venimi, ellora verum aut et expel ipsame doluptatio eiusape llaturitia quos alit, optat in ent ape lit hari vit, commodis inverior anduciet harcit que volestium fuga. Officiam aut ipsum inulliquo in et quis sa aut vel ma quoditi anteceatur suntur modi

Baskerville Regular
11 pt type, 16 pt leading (11/16)
Listio venimi, ellora verum aut et expel ipsame doluptatio eiusape llaturitia quos alit, optat in ent ape lit hari vit, commodis inverior anduciet harcit que volestium fuga. Officiam aut ipsum inulliquo in et quis sa aut vel ma quoditi anteceatur suntur modi

Myriad Pro Condensed
11 pt type, 15 pt leading (11/16)
Listio venimi, ellora verum aut et expel ipsame doluptatio eiusape llaturitia quos alit, optat in ent ape lit hari vit, commodis inverior anduciet harcit que volestium fuga. Officiam aut ipsum inulliquo in et quis sa aut vel ma quoditi anteceatur suntur modi

Use ample leading, also called line spacing

Leading is the space between lines. Do not use "Auto" which adds 20 percent between lines; 11-point type would have 13.2-point autoleading. Leading of 30 percent should be the minimum for book text, although the InDesign default is 20 percent. Leading of 30 percent for 11-point type is 14.3-point leading. I use 11/16 for this book. Use 120 to 145 percentof the font size.

Using the reader-friendly examples on the previous page, the same text has leading set to Auto. It looks too cramped and cannot breathe. The previous "Correct" examples with 11-pt with 16-pt leading is easier to read.

Examples of too tight leading:

Too Tight

Century Gothic Regular
11 pt type,13.2 pt leading (11/13.2)
Listio venimi, ellora verum aut et expel ipsame doluptatio eiusape llaturitia quos alit, optat in ent ape lit hari vit, commodis inverior anduciet harcit que volestium fuga. Officiam aut ipsum inulliquo in et quis sa aut vel ma quoditi anteceatur suntur modi

Baskerville Regular
11 pt type,13.2 pt leading (11/13.2)
Listio venimi, ellora verum aut et expel ipsame doluptatio eiusape llaturitia quos alit, optat in ent ape lit hari vit, commodis inverior anduciet harcit que volestium fuga. Officiam aut ipsum inulliquo in et quis sa aut vel ma quoditi anteceatur suntur modi

Myriad Pro Condensed
11 pt type,13.2 pt leading (11/13.2)
Listio venimi, ellora verum aut et expel ipsame doluptatio eiusape llaturitia quos alit, optat in ent ape lit hari vit, commodis inverior anduciet harcit que volestium fuga. Officiam aut ipsum inulliquo in et quis sa aut vel ma quoditi anteceatur suntur modi

Make the length of the line comfortable to read

There are varying rules as to the length of a line. The range is typically about 65–70 characters per line, including spaces. Adjust the line length, margins, and text type size of 10- to 12-point for book design to this standard.

Typeface size and use

Evaluate the size and structure of the characters in a typeface before committing to it. Make sure the type size can be easy to read in headlines or body text.

This is 24-point Ambroise Std Light. It is a gorgeous font in large headlines for print or online.

ExtraBold is used for this book's title, Book Design...

This is Ambroise Std Light in 10-point type. It becomes harder to read. What is happening? The light lines in the structure of the characters are reduced, so it seems like the letters almost disappear when used at this size. Before finalizing any typeface for body text or a headline, print out a sample page.

Tracking adjusted

The first example shows 100+ added tracking. A bit of tracking in the headline widens the letterspacing and gives the headline a different look. It is not advisable for body text.

    The middle example is typeset with no tracking. In the last example, tracking is set to -50. Letters that touch should be avoided. The text is too tight to be easily read.

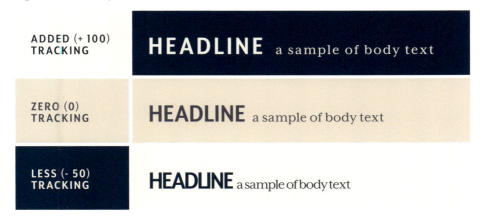

CHAPTER ONE | DESIGN FUNDAMENTALS   19

Do not skimp on white space!

Body text that runs the width of a page is difficult for the eyes to follow across the page. Try using two or three columns instead. Compare two examples below. The same text in the first example is also used in the second example. The latter is not only much easier to read, but is also more attractive.

- Resist the temptation to make the text type larger than 11.5- to 12-point.
- Do not kill white space by making the page margins narrower.
- Adding two returns between paragraphs adds too much space.

Weak   This is an example of page with a line length that is hard to read comfortably. The example has a full return between paragraphs which is too much space.

Better   The same text set in two columns with ample white space and margins.

Consistent text paragraph styles

Establish a Paragraph Style and use it throughout the book. You can use one of the following two styles. *Either:*

- Indent the first line of each paragraph, or
- Use one return between paragraphs. Type the enter key once. It is better to use some space, but less than a full return.

Note that there is no indent in the first paragraph of a chapter or section. Use *one* of these two examples as they are both correct.

Indent OPTION 1: Indented paragraphs with no space between.

Ehendit alicatem rehenducimi, comnis soluptatent quae ero optaqui optio del maximus maionsediti ulliqui doluptiam.

Il et perunt occum fugit eos et a con cuptaes aut aut vitione expel expeliandit eos rest, cus, ut estrumq uatur, simus acea veles doluptio ipsunt occab incto excestiamus voluptatem ium.

Cus eicipie necerro rumquas ditatem. Hitibus. Officipsam, corepediam cuptistia consectotat que voluptate poruptatur? Sitio cuptate ndignima nobitia incturi berumque dolupid que.

One return OPTION 2: Paragraphs with one return. Hit the "enter" key once.

Ehendit alicatem rehenducimi, comnis soluptatent quae ero optaqui optio del maximus maionsediti ulliqui doluptiam.

Il et perunt occum fugit eos et a con cuptaes aut aut vitione expel expeliandit eos rest, cus, ut estrumq uatur, simus acea veles doluptio ipsunt occab incto excestiamus voluptatem ium.

Cus eicipie necerro rumquas ditatem. Hitibus. Officipsam, corepediam cuptistia consectotat que voluptate poruptatur? Sitio cuptate ndignima nobitia incturi berumque dolupid que.

Use one space between sentences, not two

The rule in typing class is to put two spaces between sentences. Typesetting is different. Use one space between sentences in a paragraph.

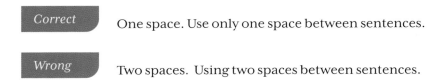

One space. Use only one space between sentences.

Two spaces. Using two spaces between sentences.

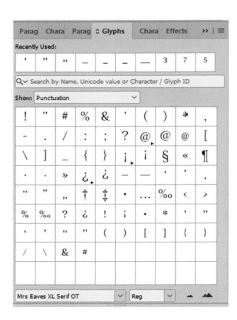

Use typographer's quotes

Do not use straight quotes or prime marks in place of professional "Typographer's Quotes." They are also called "curly quotes", and can be generated automatically.

Go to Edit > Preferences > Type. Check the "Typographer's Quotes" box because the default is the straight mark.

When typesetting inches or feet, use straight marks. Quote marks can be selected by going to Glyphs > Punctuation.

" " quote use	"Typographer's Quotes" in body text
" inches	typeset the prime mark for 12" (inches)
' feet	use the prime mark for 1' (foot)

To select a glyph, go to Glyphs in the Typography panel or type Alt + Shift + F11, then select Punctuation.

Make sure that you are working in the correct typeface as shown in the lower left corner of the illustration above. The font style can also be seen to the right of the typeface.

22   BOOK DESIGN: SIMPLE & PROFESSIONAL

Overused typefaces

An often-made mistake is to use a typeface that comes preloaded on the computer or just used too often. If you are working in Adobe InDesign on a subscription basis, you likely have access to Adobe Fonts. *Use them!*

Listed below are some of the most frequently used fonts that we suggest you do *not* use. They are among the preloaded fonts on your computer or are overused typefaces.

Overused / Preloaded

Arial	Georgia	Times New Roman
Bradley Hand	Helvetica	TRAJAN
Comic Sans	Impact	Viner Hand
Courier	Kristen	Vivaldi
Franklin Gothic	Papyrus	Zapfino
Futura		

Script and handwriting capitalization

Capitalizing the primary words in script and handwriting typefaces is most often easier to read. All uppercase letters usually does not work.

The examples in the left column are set in uppercase and are hard to read. The same typefaces are then set in upper- and lowercase. These are great typefaces, but hard to read in all uppercase.

Incorrect Uppercase

TOO HARD TO READ	Easy to Read
TOO HARD TO READ	Easy to Read
TOO HARD TO READ	Easy to Read
TOO HARD TO READ	Easy to Read
TOO HARD TO READ	Easy to Read

Widows and Orphans

Orphan

Lorem ipsum dolor sit amet, consectetur adipisicing elit, sed do eiusmod tempor incididunt ut labore et dolore magna aliqua.

Ut enim ad minim veniam, quis nostrud exercitation ullamco laboris nisi ut aliquip ex ea commodo consequat. Duis aute irure dolor in reprehenderit in voluptate velit esse cillum dolore eu fugiat nulla pariatur.

Excepteur sint occaecat cupidatat non proident, sunt in culpa qui officia deserunt mollit anim id est laborum.

Sed ut perspiciatis unde omnis iste natus error sit voluptatem accusantium doloremque laudantium, totam rem aperiam, eaque ipsa quae ab illo inventore veritatis et quasi architecto beatae vitae dicta sunt explicabo.

Nemo enim ipsam voluptatem quia voluptas sit aspernatur aut odit aut fugit, sed quia consequuntur magni dolores eos

nesciunt.

Duis aute irure dolor in reprehenderit in voluptate velit esse cillum dolore eu fugiat nulla pariatur.

Excepteur sint occaecat cupidatat non proident, sunt in culpa qui officia deserunt mollit anim id est laborum. Sed ut perspiciatis unde omnis iste natus error sit voluptatem accusantium doloremque laudantium, totam rem aperiam, eaque ipsa quae ab illo inventore veritatis et quasi architecto beatae vitae dicta sunt explicabo.

Lorem ipsum dolor sit amet, consectetur adipisicing elit, sed do eiusmod tempor incididunt ut labore et dolore magna aliqua. Ut enim ad minim veniam, quis nostrud exercitation ullamco laboris nisi ut aliquip ex ea commodo consequat. Duis aute irure dolor in reprehenderit in voluptate velit esse cillum dolore eu fugiat nulla pariatur.

Excepteur sint occaecat cupidatat non

Widows

WIDOW

A *short line or single word* at the *end* of a paragraph. Avoid by editing text or modifying spacing to lengthen or lose the line. A single word in the widow example on the example's left page is permissible but avoid if possible.

ORPHAN

A *word, or part of a word* appearing alone at the *end* of a paragraph which is at the *top* of a page or column. Orphans should be avoided by rewording or changing the spacing to lengthen or shorten a line.

Ladders

We expect words to be hyphenated. However, when two or more subsequent lines of type are hyphenated, we see "ladders." It is a an unwanted distraction for the reader in addition to being a typographical eyesore. There is a better way to eliminate many hyphens. When hyphenated words occur, adjust the type to correct ladders, as seen in the four lines indicated in this paragraph.

Uncheck the hyphenation box for the body text style or adjust Paragraph Style Options > Hyphenation. The body text in this book is "Left Justify." If it were set to "Left," the right side of the text would be ragged,

24   BOOK DESIGN: SIMPLE & PROFESSIONAL

meaning each line of type would not go all the way to the right edge. It is easier to work with Left versus Left Justify, but justified text is a great look for body text, particularly in novels.

To turn off hyphenation, go to Paragraph Styles. Either change the "body text" style that you created or go to [Basic Paragraph] and change all styles based on the [Basic Paragraph] style. Double-click your named style, and the Paragraph Style Options window opens. Select Hyphenation on the left side and uncheck the box for hyphenation.

When there is need of a hyphen, type it in. For a discretionary hyphen that is only visible when needed, right click the mouse, go to Insert Special Character, then go to Hyphens and Dashes. Select Discretionary Hyphen. The short cut is Ctrl + Shift + - for a discretionary hyphen.

Hanging quotes

When setting a hanging quote or hanging punctuation, only the left double quotation mark is moved to the left of a standalone text block. A *hanging* quote mark does not appear in the body text.

The following is how a hanging quote should look. The text is enlarged to better show the alignment of the text with the hanging quotation mark.

Correct

"The way we're running the company,

the product design, the advertising,

it all comes down to this:

Let's make it simple. Really simple."

—STEVE JOBS

Wrong

"The way we're running the company,

the product design, the advertising,

it all comes down to this:

Let's make it simple. Really simple."

—STEVE JOBS

En and em dashes instead of hyphens

HYPHEN " - "

A hyphen is used in the normal course of typing and hyphenates words. It resides on the same key with the underscore " _ ". Avoid two letter hyphenations in the last word at the end of a paragraph, like " -ed " or " -ly ."

EN DASH " – "

When there is a duration or connection as used in numbers, time, or months, an en dash is used instead of a hyphen. It is best to use the word "to", but an en dash looks better in charts, for example.

Add one thin space before and after the en dash. In some typefaces the en dash may touch the adjacent characters. This should be avoided. Kerning is another option.

Type an en dash: Alt + -

En dash set correctly

An estimated 100–125 people were at the wedding.

The class will be 9–10:30 a.m. beginning tomorrow.

Our school year is August–June because of heavy winter snow.

EM DASH " — "

An em dash may be used once or twice, but do not use it three times in a sentence. A pair of em dashes is used to set off an explanatory statement. The em dash pair is also used in a sentence to eliminate too many commas. A run-on sentence should be edited by the author.

Contrary to what is done with the en dash, do not add space on either side of an em dash. Slight kerning may be used if the letters touch. Touching letters will vary among typefaces. The words on either side of the em dash should be close to the em dash.

Type an em dash: Alt + Shift + -

Em dash set correctly

The duchess—who was not available for comment—was on her way to attend the ceremony, but arrived fifty minutes late to the event.

Ellipsis typeset

While it is easy to use an ellipsis that is a three-dot character in a typeface, it looks better when it is built. Adding a space between three periods looks too spaced out. It is not only the spacing that should be corrected, but when adding a space between three periods, the line could break and a period or two could flow to the next line.

There can be a difference too in how to a set an ellipsis as it appears in different typefaces. This is yet another reason why classic, professional typefaces are the best choice for body text. Depending on the source, there is not just one way to fix the spacing in ellipses.

CREATE YOUR OWN ELLIPSES

Use periods. Use a "Nonbreaking Space" for the spaces between periods or thin spaces. Use the correct examples.

Correct

Setting type . . . an ellipsis.
space, **period**, thin space, **period**, thin space, **period**, space

Setting type . . . an ellipsis.
space, **period**, non-breaking space, **period**, non-breaking space, **period**, space

Setting type...an ellipsis.
ellipsis character, no spaces on either side of ellipsis

Wrong

Setting type . . . an ellipsis.
space, **period**, space, **period**, space, **period**, space

Setting type ... an ellipsis.
space, **period**, **period**, **period**, space

Words over the same words

I avoided starting this paragraph with the same words over same words in the headline. Stay clear of words on words in paragraphs and in headlines with the first words in the paragraph.

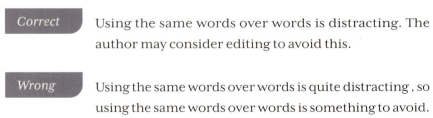

Correct

Using the same words over words is distracting. The author may consider editing to avoid this.

Wrong

Using the same words over words is quite distracting , so using the same words over words is something to avoid.

Add tracking to small type

Smaller type sizes look better with a bit of tracking (kerning) is added. If a type size is smaller than the body text, it may benefit from adding tracking; anywhere from + 5 to + 50. *Examples:*

The 8-point size text on the copyright page has + 5 tracking added.

Copyright © 2021 by Nancy Starkman.
All rights reserved. This book may not be reproduced or utilized in any form or by any means, electronic or mechanical, including photography, recording, or by any information storage and retrieval system, without permission in writing from the author.
All photographs and images are used with permission.

The smaller text of 5.5 point has + 20 tracking added.

BOOK DESIGN: SIMPLE & PROFESSIONAL IS NOT AUTHORIZED, ENDORSED OR SPONSORED BY ADOBE, PUBLISHER OF ADOBE INDESIGN, ADOBE PHOTOSHOP, ADOBE ACROBAT, ADOBE ILLUSTRATOR, AND ADOBE FONTS. Adobe, InDesign, Photoshop, Acrobat, Illustrator, Adobe Camera Raw, Adobe Fonts, Garamond Premier Pro, Jensen, Kepler, Minion, Myriad, Trajan, and Warnock are registered trademarks or trademarks of Adobe Inc., which is incorporated in the United States and other countries. Microsoft, Windows, Word and Excel are registered trademarks of Microsoft Corporation. Pantone, Pantone Matching System, Pantone Color Bridge, Pantone Fan Chip, PMS, Pantone Colors, Pantone Names, numbers, formulas, or trademarks or copyrights of Pantone LLC. *Book Design: Simple & Professional* is an independent book and has not been authorized, sponsored, or otherwise approved by Apple Inc. Apple®, Mac®, and [. . .]

Captions are often small and should have added kerning or tracking. The amount of kerning depends on the typeface. Avoid using horizontal or even vertical scale as a substitution for kerning. It only skews and distorts the well-formed characters of high-quality fonts.

Safe margins

Star Print Brokers does not use "safe" margins as we only print high-quality books. But that is not universally true. Some POD or print-on-demand services require a safe margin of up to a quarter inch.

POD services usually need a safe margin as they are outputting single pages from an output device. The pages can be jostled around which can sometimes happen with a desktop printer.

TO BREATHE OR BLEED

It does not look good to set text close to the trim. Print out and trim a page to evaluate. Either give text and images room to breathe or let then bleed.

Check with your printer as you want to avoid unnecessary and time-consuming file changes.

Bleeds

To bleed means to print an image over the edge of a sheet or page and then trim after printing. A bleed is usually 3 mm, or 1/8 inch (0.125 inch).

COST TO BLEED

At Star Print Brokers, there is no difference in cost when printing in Asia, if clients want to print with bleeds. It is best to have a final quote from the chosen printer before beginning the design.

Printers in the USA frequently charge more for a book that has bleeds or even heavy ink coverage. The quality is lower in the USA and the cost is higher than with our select printers. We print with a handful of trusted providers with whom we have worked nearly two decades. They do not have factories in China. We never print in China.

HOW TO BLEED AN IMAGE

A bleed is most often 1/8 inch; that is 3 mm or 0.125 inch. To set up bleeds for any document in InDesign, go to File > Document Set-up . . . and click Bleed and Slug. Then enter the bleed. See Chapter 5, *Interior Pages*, page 93.

If you need to switch between millimeters and inches, go to Edit > Preferences > Units & Increments . . . and under Ruler Units type in the measurement under both Horizontal and Vertical. See Chapter 6, *Cover Design & Binding*, page 110.

Bolder, bigger, or not

Quite often there is a tendency to add more emphasis to some part of the designed page. We run into even more problems when the page is revised several times and becomes too cluttered, too bold, too overbearing.

The design soon looks like almost everything is made bigger, bolder, more color is added, and so on. It is gawdy.

The solution is to reevaluate all the elements on the page. It is better design to have less, so bigger, bolder text or headlines serve a purpose. Calm down the page by using body text in Regular. Consider changing any Bold type to Regular, or downsizing some type, so other type can stand out.

Copyright page text should be smaller than the body text of the book. There is no functional purpose in making the copyright text bold.

Avoid the temptation to make a headline or an element bolder or bigger. Instead, leave the headline alone and lighten up or reduce the size of other typeset elements. *Simplify!*

Alignment

Alignment in book design should be consistent. Establish the body text and headline alignment by creating Paragraph Styles. Clean up ragged paragraphs manually or with hyphenation.

JUSTIFICATION FOR BODY TEXT

The alignment to use for most body text is Left or Left Justify. The difference between them is the last line of the paragraph. Use Left Justify for the entire paragraph, or the last line will be awkwardly spread across the text block.

JUSTIFICATION FOR HEADLINES

Utilitarian book headlines versus headlines or subheads for a special use, are most commonly Left or Center. Avoid Full Justify, so your headlines do not look like this:

Avoid   "Full   Justify"   for   Headlines

The alignment of this title and text is "Left Justify"

Rem id mo beror rempore stiunt abo. Rumqui offictemquos modis dundes ero voluptasit aut omnis alitia cum eos moluptatum quae occus, quaera sundis et quia nus discia doluptia quam, sed explabo restrunto maiostios culpa id modi re et lit rem ium la nos eos sit, aboraec taquae.

The alignment of this title and text is "Full Justify"

Rem id mo beror rempore stiunt abo. Rumqui offictemquos modis dundes ero voluptasit aut omnis alitia cum eos moluptatum quae occus, quaera sundis et quia nus discia doluptia quam, sed explabo restrunto maiostios culpa id modi re et lit rem ium la nos eos sit, aboraec taquae.

The alignment of this title and text is "Left"

Rem id mo beror rempore stiunt abo. Rumqui offictemquos modis dundes ero voluptasit aut omnis alitia cum eos moluptatum quae occus, quaera sundis et quia nus discia doluptia quam, sed explabo restrunto maiostios culpa id modi re et lit rem ium la nos eos sit, aboraec taquae.

The alignment of this title and text is "Right"

Rem id mo beror rempore stiunt abo. Rumqui offictemquos modis dundes ero voluptasit aut omnis alitia cum eos moluptatum quae occus, quaera sundis et quia nus discia doluptia quam, sed explabo restrunto maiostios culpa id modi re et lit rem ium la nos eos sit, aboraec taquae.

The alignment of this title and text is "Center Justify"

Rem id mo beror rempore stiunt abo. Rumqui officemquos modis dundes ero voluptasit aut omnis alitia cum eos moluptatum quae occus, quaera sundis et quia nus discia doluptia quam, sed explabo restrunto maiostios culpa id modi re et lit rem ium la nos eos sit, aboraec taquae.

The alignment of this title and text is "Center"

Rem id mo beror rempore stiunt abo. Rumqui officemquos modis dundes ero voluptasit aut omnis alitia cum eos moluptatum quae occus, quaera sundis et quia nus discia doluptia quam, sed explabo restrunto maiostios culpa id modi re et lit rem ium la nos eos sit, aboraec taquae.

Centered text is more difficult for the eye to follow. Save it for special uses, but not for the body text of a book.

Apostrophes, right- and left-facing

An apostrophe used correctly indicates something to be replaced that is missing. The 19 in 1970s is replaced by a left-facing apostrophe. Additionally, there is no apostrophy between "70" and "s" because '70s is not possessive in this use.

The incorrect example is what is automatically typed in most applications other than InDesign.

Correct   **He went to school in the '70s.**

Wrong   **He went to school in the '70's.**

- Preferences for better book design
- Standard book sizes
- Paper stock
- Choosing typefaces
- Selecting a color scheme
- Working with color in text
- Page margins
- Book page layout
- Cover considerations
- Manuscript and captions
- Collecting photos and images
- Resolution for book printing
- Actual and effective resolution
- Author & designer responsibilities

PLANNING A BOOK
Vision and Process

HAVE A PLAN AND CREATE A STYLE. Investigate books with similar subject matter. Compare the manufacturing quality, design, type of binding, page count, dimensions, and retail price. Can you charge more or less than other books? The more books you print means the lower the unit cost.

When thinking about the book plan, consider the type and style of book that you are publishing. A novel for example, may be the easiest book to plan. It is mostly text, and perhaps simple black and white line drawings, or a few photos. The real consideration is the cover. It needs to convey the right message to sell books.

Another example, a cookbook, can be simple or complex in design. It will have formatted recipes and possibly charts. A cookbook needs a unique style. There are many food-related subjects to write about, including cuisine, wine, and diet. The cookbook cover is just as important as for a novel. Photos of food must look delicious, so that the reader wants to buy the book.

Have a vision in mind. Look for inspiration for better book design as creativity can take a book to the next level. Better design can sell more books.

QUICK TIPS

- Get a book printing quote before you finalize a plan. Dimensions might be adjusted to reduce cost. Could the book be made larger for the same printing cost? Is shipping cost affected?
- Select typefaces, use of color, and page layout. This includes master pages, paragraph styles, and the color palette in CMYK.
- Images need to be in CMYK, not RGB. They should be at 300 ppi *and* at the size they will be when printed, or larger.
- Add an extra 0.125 inch or 3-millimeter bleed.
- Work from the manuscript in a Microsoft Word document. Image names should be referenced when working with text.

Photo by Alexandru Acea on Unsplash

Preferences for Adobe InDesign

Please start with the default Adobe InDesign settings. Having said that, there is a number of changes to make to the default InDesign settings. This is not required but makes for better looking typography.

More tweaks can be made than what is listed here. Some of the adjustments depend on the typefaces that are selected as part of the design for the book. You want to keep your work "simple & professional," so this is a partial list.

SETTINGS FOR ONE BOOK DESIGN DOCUMENT

If you are primarily designing books, then either open InDesign without creating a document or close all documents if InDesign is already open. Set the following suggested defaults. All documents that you create will have these settings.

SETTINGS FOR ALL DOCUMENTS

If InDesign will be used to design projects other than books, then create the first document for your book and apply these settings. Save the file and use it as the basis for the rest of the chapters or documents in your book.

When the book and book documents are closed and you open InDesign again, the original default settings will still be there.

SUGGESTED SETTINGS

- Tighten Kerning. Go to Edit > Preferences > Units & Increments (Windows), see the Kerning. Preferences > Units & Increments (Mac). Under "Keyboard Increments" change "Kerning / Tracking" to 5 / 1000 em from 20 / 1000 em.
- Paragraph Styles and Character Styles should have Kerning set to Metrics. If there are very few kerning pairs in a font, you can select Optical rather than Metric. If Metric spacing does not look right, try Optical.
- Tracking is set to 0. There are many reasons to adjust tracking. When type is set in a small point size, add tracking so that the letters do not look like they are touching. A headline in all uppercase, rather than lowercase, may look great when tracking is expanded to 100, 200, or more depending on the typeface, weight, size, and use.
- Hyphenation can be adjusted under the Paragraph Style, in Hyphenation. The Hyphenation Zone should set to be 0.5 inches, 12.7 mm, or 3p0 picas, depending on whether you prefer to work in inches, millimeters, or picas.

Standard book sizes

There are standard book sizes, but many sizes are in frequent use by book printers and print-on-demand service providers. Star Print Brokers prints nearly any size book. The maximum width is 12 inches by 15 inches in length.

DIMENSIONS, ALWAYS WIDTH BY LENGTH

A book is measured by width and then length. The width is called out first. Some say "8.5" x 11" landscape." It is correct to say 11" x 8.5" for a landscape-oriented book. The orientations are portrait (vertical), landscape (horizontal), or square.

A list of book sizes for specific types of books is set by the provider you choose. The following book sizes are incomplete as sizes vary by provider.

BASIC BOOK DIMENSIONS

Digest	5.5" x 8.5"	(140 x 216 mm)
US Trade	6" x 9"	(152 x 229 mm)
Small Square	7.5" x 7.5"	(191 x 191 mm)
Square	8.5" x 8.5"	(216 x 216 mm)
Graphic Novel	6.625" x 10.25"	(168 x 260 mm)
US Letter	8.5" x 11"	(216 x 280 mm)

GUIDANCE FOR BOOK DIMENSIONS

• Determine the dimensions of the book before it is designed. Making a mistake on book size means moving text and images around on a larger or smaller page size. It takes time, possibly money, and the book may not turn out as well as in the previous layout. When changes are made, proofread again for new mistakes.

• Research other same style or types of books. Look at physical books in a bookstore or review book dimensions on Amazon.

• Get quotes or pricing from service providers or printers with whom you intend to print. Use their specifications once dimensions are final.

• Take handling costs, postal regulations, and postage into consideration. Is a fulfillment center, mail house, Amazon, or author mailing the books?

• When filling mail orders, what size plain envelope, bubble envelope, bumper box, or postal box will you use for the book?

• Charge extra for postage and handling, instead of cutting into your own profit margin.

Hardcover versus soft cover dimensions

SOFT COVER BOOK DIMENSIONS

The dimensions of a soft cover or paperback book are straight forward in terms of the text block after the cover is applied. If the interior page size of the text block is 5.5" x 8.5", then the cover is affixed and trimmed to the same size. The dimensions of the book are still 5.5" x 8.5".

There are standard sizes that vary among service providers. Check with your provider before determining book dimensions. Most POD services offer limited sizes depending on their digital output devices for book output.

HARDCOVER BOOK DIMENSIONS

We will use the same example as the interior page text block; 5.5" x 8.5". The hard case of a hardcover book holds the text block. Because the hard case boards are larger than the text block, the dimensions of the bound book are slightly larger than 5.5" x 8.5".

We still describe the dimensions of this hardcover book as 5.5" x 8.5" even though the hardcover case is larger.

The increased hard case size can differ among manufacturers. Do not assume anything! The size can be different not only from manufacturer to manufacturer, but from country to country. Fortunately, you do not have to worry about this until designing the cover wrap of a hardcover book, and if you choose to have a standard dust jacket or French fold dust jacket.

Before finalizing the cover design, the total page count and thickness of the paper needs to be determined for the spine width. See the service provider's quote or talk to their representative. They can advise you of the spine width and measurements for your InDesign files.

Print-on-Demand (POD) dimensions

POD services are most often outputting books a page or two at a time, and a few copies at a time. Dimensions vary among these services. They are limited, especially with coffee table or photography book dimensions, or when self-publishers want larger books or custom sizing. Before committing, check book dimensions, paper finishes, and paper weights with the POD provider.

DIMENSIONS ARE GAUGED BY THE OUTPUT DEVICE CAPABILITY

POD providers may offer one-off books, but they need to match book dimensions to their output devices. Pages are output with toner as with desktop copiers. Pages can smear when wiped with a moist finger. Output devices use toner just like a copier. It is not practical to print only one book with real printing ink, in signatures, and on a commercial printing press.

POD is never high-quality. A printing press requires set-ups and is high-quality book printing—at least it is with our company.

POD PRINTING IN SIGNATURES IS LIMITED OR NON-EXISTENT

A signature is a large sheet of paper stock that is printed, for example, with four pages one side and four pages on the other side to make an 8-page signature. The signature size depends on the page dimension and paper weight. A coffee table book with large dimensions may be printed in 8-page signatures, while a standard novel may print in 16-page signatures. See page 138 in Chapter 8 *Printing on Press* for a diagram of a signature.

Signatures are folded and folded again to make up booklets that are "married" together to form the text block. Professional printers need to make sure the signatures are not too thick with too many pages, or that the paper is too thick for the number of pages. One of the ways to judge a poorly bound book is to look at the top of the spine of a bound book. You should not see wide gathered signatures.

Some POD providers can do short runs on press. This is not a high-quality option. Fine printing is more than printing on just any press. Printing staff, as well, must be more than just knowledgeable about running a press.

When a self-publisher has a soft cover book and color is not important, POD is not a bad option depending on the binding. It used to be that pages would easily fall out of a soft cover book because single pages were not glued well enough. The glued binding is better with some providers than it was a few years ago. Ask for a sample book to verify the binding.

SMYTH SEWING IS LIMITED OR NON-EXISTENT AT A POD PROVIDER

Consider the page count and thickness of a book. A glued book cannot hold a great number of pages. The pages should be Smyth Sewn, but print-on-demand providers do not typically sew books. They may side-stitch (staple) the text block. That is when viewing type too close to the gutter becomes a problem. Even worse, the middle of a two-page spread will be cut-off in the gutter. So much for that beautiful two-page spread in your children's book.

Because everything is structured and mass produced at POD services, self-publishers have to use the POD provider's standard book sizes. Again, sizes differ among service providers. Print-on-demand books and their dimensions are generally driven by paper sizes as they output—not print on press—one or two pages at a time.

POD CUSTOM BOOK DIMENSIONS ARE LIMITED OR NON-EXISTENT

Self-publishers may need non-standard sizes. Star Print Brokers often prints 12" x 12" books and other large-format book sizes. All books are printed on press, in signatures. We also print landscape-oriented books in hardcover or soft cover. There are fewer restrictions than with POD services.

Our maximum text block size is 12 inches wide by 15 inches in length. Occasionally, someone requests a landscape-orientation book that is not long enough for the width. The final hard case bound book would torque. Clients are advised of a better length for the width, while maintaining the landscape orientation.

Paper stock

Our company's coated and uncoated stocks are acid-free archival paper.

COATED PAPER AT SPB

This paper stock has a clay coating on the surface and is used for the finest book printing including coffee table books, art books, and photography books. It is also for children's picture books because it stays somewhat cleaner with constant use than uncoated stock and reflects superior color.

- Matte coated paper comes in a variety of weights.
- Gloss coated paper is also available in a selection of weights, but is a bit thinner than matte of the same weight.

UNCOATED PAPER AT SPB

Paperback novels and inexpensive books that are not meant to last for years. For uncoated stock is a good choice. Our stock is named "woodfree."

- Woodfree stock is uncoated and is available in a selection of paper weights. We advise clients about weights and finishes for particular types of books and printing.

Choosing typefaces

Type combinations for book design is a subject of great interest to book designers and self-publishing authors. Always select typefaces for a professional look, to complement the style or theme of the book.

A brief introduction to using type

Fonts have different extensions and are most commonly .OTF or .TTF or PostScript fonts. Do not use any other fonts types.

- Open Type Fonts (.OTF) are widely used cross-platform fonts. It is easier to share files across operating systems. If given a choice, select .OTF.
- TrueType Font and Post Script are also font extensions.

There are so many type combinations and possibilities. We are limiting the discussion to just provide basic user information.

Font pairs

A typeface is a family of fonts that may be paired. Typeface families are paired with great care. There are typeface and font combinations that you may already own, or can download for free. If you subscribe to Adobe to use InDesign, you have access to all the Adobe Fonts for as long as you subscribe.

What if you do not have Adobe® Fonts®? Google® Fonts® and Font Squirrel® are also sources for free fonts. MyFonts® is a good place to buy fonts or go directly to designer and foundry websites.

There are always new typefaces on the market. Be wary of using free or cheap, one-off typefaces for body text, but they might work for headlines. The body text typeface is the real workhorse, so use a classic typeface for body text, but not one that is overused or comes preloaded on the computer.

The spacing can be off on typefaces created by amateur designers. The set text may look awkward which is another reason to use a classic font.

I often polish books for clients. Recently, I ran into a problem with an adorable, yet obscure font by an unknown designer. I noticed that the uppercase "P" next to a lowercase "a" had too much space between the letters. The kerning was set to Metrics. I changed it to Optical and expanded the tracking to +10 to match the width of the word when it was in Metrics. I corrected all the headlines. It would have been easier if the self-publisher had used a Paragraph Style. The change could have been made globally or in one document, and then synchronized with the rest of the book.

Metric kerning is the default to use, but if letter spacing looks off, switch to Optical kerning. There is debate about Metric versus Optical, but this works for me.

If you are not familiar with the classic typefaces suitable for book text, use Adobe Fonts or invest in a classic typeface family. The standard font styles to choose for each typeface are Regular, *Italic*, **Bold**, and ***Bold Italic***.

Pairing fonts for book design

SUPERFAMILIES

A superfamily comprises typefaces that can be grouped together because they share the same basic style. Examples are Helvetica and Helvetica Narrow. Typefaces that have both serif and sans serif fonts, like Mr Eaves and Mrs Eaves also form a superfamily.

SAME TYPEFACE, DIFFERENT FONTS

One way to pair is to use fonts from the same typeface family for both body copy and headlines. Most often body text would be 10- or 11-point. The largest headlines are quite often in the Bold font and have significantly more contrast compared to the text. Design subheads with hierarchy in mind.

Additionally, the same size typeface may be used throughout. However, adjust uppercase and letterspacing (kerning) for headlines. Linespacing or the leading between lines can also be adjusted for minimalistic style.

COMBINE A SANS SERIF WITH A SERIF TYPEFACE

This is the most popular way to pair fonts. The body text can be a serif typeface with a sans serif headline, or the other way around. The styles should be compatible, having a similar x-height and using contrast.

CONTRAST

Large and small type

Use contrast for headlines and body text. Notice the high and low contrast of the letter "B" in the example on the following page. A bolder headline conveys contrast. Make sure that the weight is strong enough to give the headline the contrast it needs next to the body text.

Font color and its background color

Contrast may be the font color and the background on which it appears. Adding color can provide the needed contrast.

Typeface contrast

Contrast should be utilized between different typefaces. A nice script font for headlines paired with a sans serif font for body text is an example. The combination works especially well for cookbook recipe pages.

X-HEIGHT DEFINITION

The x-height is the distance from the baseline to the top of a lowercase letter that has no ascenders or descenders: c, e, m, n, o, r, s, u, v, w, x, z.

ESTABLISH THE HIERARCHY WITH FONT WEIGHTS AND SIZE

Headlines are quite often larger than body text and that is a way to establish hierarchy. Also make sure that the weight is strong enough to give the headline the contrast it needs next to the body text.

MATCH THE MOOD

Do the typefaces play well together? Read typeface descriptions when possible. If one typeface is described as "techy" and the other as "vintage," it probably is not a good idea to combine them as pairs.

TWO SERIFS OR TWO SANS SERIF TYPEFACES DO NOT MIX

Using two different typefaces from different families for headline and text is most often a mistake. For instance, do not use the serif typeface Palatino with Garamond, or another serif type. The same holds true for two different sans serif typefaces from different families.

TYPEFACES OF THE SAME CLASSIFICATION ARE A NO-GO

An example is combining a slab serif heading with another slab serif typeface for text. However, you could use the slab serif typeface, Rockwell Bold, in a headline, with Rockwell Regular for the body text.

Typefaces and paper stock

Consider the paper before making font selections. We use coated and uncoated paper. Our Uncoated paper is fairly smooth, but if the book is printed elsewhere, they may use a rougher stock with a greater absorption than our Woodfree Uncoated. Ask the provider for a paper sample.

A WORD OF CAUTION ABOUT SOME POD UNCOATED STOCK

A complaint about uncoated stock from a POD or low-cost printer is often the rough feel. However, our uncoated stock's smooth finish is nice to touch.

Paper effecting typefaces

The lesson here is if printing on poor quality uncoated stock using a large, heavy headline font, the ink could bleed so that the type looks slightly fuzzy. This is not desirable.

Neue Aachen Pro Bold, is a lovely font, but poorly executed. The "Wrong" example is printed in a book from my library.

Star Print Brokers' uncoated stock is not rough, unlike most cheap stock. *Book Design: Simple & Professional* is printed on coated stock.

The "Wrong" example is printed on a rough, uncoated stock. The leading and kerning are too tight, with (minus) -30 tracking, accentuating the issue. Letters should not touch. An exception is if letters touching is part of a style which could be the case in a logo. However, letters that are so close together look more like a mistake that should certainly be avoided in book text or headlines.

Wrong

This is an example of manipulating a font so that it would NOT print well, especially on an uncoated paper.

Correct

This is an example of the same font that would print well, and especially on an uncoated paper.

Selecting a color scheme

Color schemes can go wrong if both CMYK and RGB are not understood. RGB is made from colored light to provide a wider color array.

CMYK is more limited in its array. If you want the website and book colors to match, or you do not want to be surprised at what you see printed on press, then follow this advice.

CMYK FOR PRINT, RGB FOR SCREENS, HTML FOR WEB

If selecting color for book printing on press and viewing an online website, select CMYK process colors first, then match RGB to CMYK. See Chapter 8 *Printing on Press*, page 141 for more about printing color on press.

BLACK—OR COLOR SWATCHES—WITH TINTS

Novels most often do not have any color other than black. If variation is needed on the page but color is not wanted or is not in the budget, make gray tints instead. Go to Swatches, put the cursor on [Black] to highlight, then go to the three horizonal lines in the upper right corner. Select "New Tint Swatch . . . " and a new window opens. See "tint" at the bottom. Type in a value of 30%. Click Add. Repeat as needed but limit the number of tints to avoid a cluttered look.

MATCHING PHOTOS WITH EYEDROPPER TOOL

There is a seemingly endless number of color combinations. If you have an image that is symbolic of the subject matter of the book, select colors from the image to add to the Swatches. The number of swatches should be limited to two to five colors. An exception may be swatches for a color-coded

Color scheme selected from the CMYK photo.

Seattle Japanese Garden, Washington Park Arboretum.
Photo by Nancy Starkman

CHAPTER TWO | PLANNING A BOOK 43

reference book where many more may colors may be needed. If matching color from an image, always start by converting the photo or image to CMYK since that is the mode that we use when printing books on press.

To convert to CMYK in Photoshop, go to File > Convert to Profile... select Destination Space. Star Print Brokers uses U.S. Sheetfed Coated v2. It could also be U.S. Sheetfed Uncoated v2, but this is not a critical difference for this task. Place the photo in the document by selecting Ctrl + D and navigate to the image's folder to select it.

While still in InDesign, use the eyedropper tool to select a color in the photo. Then go to Swatches and add the color. Repeat as needed.

The new swatches may be used for selected headlines, background color, or other areas where color is desired. The possibilities are endless. Selecting CMYK from photos is a great way to create Swatches and / or brand colors. Since RGB has the wider array, convert the CMYK color to RGB for web color. The color still might not be exact, but the chances are much greater that RGB and CMYK colors will match when selecting color using this method.

Working with color in text

Let's look at text in black, process, and spot ink. There are differences. Avoid costly printing mistakes and extra time revising your files. Often, a crucial mistake is made using black body text. It is either in black, a CMYK process color screen build, or a spot ink. It should never be in process.

BLACK INK FOR TEXT

"Black" in the InDesign Swatches palette is most often used for the book's body text.

Usually a novel or coffee table book is setup in 10-, 11- or 12-point type. The text type size is small compared to other print elements or design. Headlines and subheads are often larger than the text type size. The text is usually black.

We get into problems if text is not [black] as selected from InDesign Swatches. The other choice for text is a spot ink, but if printing a book with process color images, an additional spot ink adds to the printing cost. Never use process on small type.

BLACK INK
from single ink tray, or K tray from CMYK

One black text ink can come from a single ink tray, if printing on a 1-color press. Much of the time, books is printed on 6-color presses, using four trays of ink—cyan, magenta, yellow, and black. CMYK is process color. In this example, the ink is [black] in the swatch palette or drawn from the black tray only in printing. Do not use "Registration" black or "Rich" black.

SCREEN BUILDS IN PROCESS COLOR

Do not use Process Color for text throughout the book.

See the screen build example. A screen build is any color built from process color. A circle is imposed over the capital 'A'. When printing with CMYK, each ink screen has a different angle. We print one screen on top of the other and together they form the *rosette*, as seen in the circle.

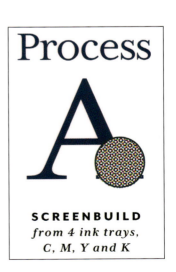

SCREENBUILD
from 4 ink trays, C, M, Y and K

You can see a slight color glow around the letter. It is the edges of the rosette. The halo will not affect large headlines depending on size and a type style. Small text in any process color will not print well on press. Check for this on physical proofs.

If the type is set up in process color, change it to 'Black' in the Swatches palette. Double check the Paragraph Styles, and Character Styles.

SPOT INK. CHANGE CMYK TO PMS INK

If you use a Spot ink, it adds a fifth ink tray to the press, and it is an additional charge.

Let's say that you are designing away and would like to change from a CMYK ink to PMS color—Pantone Matching System—for certain text styles or smaller headlines, subheads, or captions.

That means that in a typical process color book, the cost to print increases because of additional inks. Be sure of what the printing quote says before adding a Pantone spot color. Text color, using PMS inks, can be printed in process color, or a spot ink.

If you do not have full color images, you could design a book in two spot inks, for example. You may be changing the text color from CMYK to PMS text. You may choose spot black for text, and one PMS spot for a headline or decoration.

An option for a two-color book is not to use black at all. We recommend a dark PMS for one spot ink, and a contrasting ink for other elements. How about deep purple for text and a dark gold for headlines? Maybe a deep brown for text with red headlines?

You are the designer and there are many options. Technically, avoid process CMYK process color text. Instead use [Black] ink and always verify the quote if inks change. This may change the printing quote.

Note: This book is printed in process color. We did not add a fifth ink. The 'Spot A" color you see in the image on the left is printed in process color, not in spot color.

SOLID COLOR
from 1 ink tray, single or 5th tray

46 BOOK DESIGN: SIMPLE & PROFESSIONAL

InDesign Swatches palette

The beauty of the Pantone Color Bridge fan deck is that the swatches are side by side comparisons of a spot PMS (Pantone Matching System) ink (pre-mixed ink) next to the process color screenbuild (CMYK from 4 ink trays on press.) The process color is as close as one can get to the spot color. Pantone Color Bridge Coated fan deck swatches are an asset for a book designer.

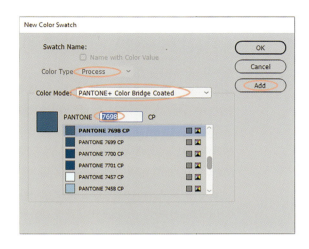

SET-UP FOR PANTONE INK

Go to Swatches. See the three horizontal lines in the top right-hand corner. Click on them and select New Color Swatch . . .

COLOR TYPE	Process
COLOR MODE	Pantone + Color Bridge Coated
PANTONE	7698 CP (replace with your choice)

Click Add. If making a change to an existing color, click OK instead.

Notice how different the spot and process versions are in these images. If planning branding or a logo that will be printed and also used online, select a PMS color where the spot and process versions match more closely. The RGB and HTML equivalents are also provided on the swatches.

The Pantone Color Bridge is great to own, and I am happy to advise our clients of any color differences if they contact me. If you are a graphic designer or book designer, you should buy the Pantone Color Bridge Coated. If you are a self-publisher, it is probably not necessary.

While we own the physical Pantone Library for print production, we use the Pantone Color Bridge Coated most often, as most of the books we print are on coated stock.

Page margins

There are quite a few graphic design books that discuss page sizes and margins. Some are confusing. For instance, often books show a diagram of a two-page spread with inner margins that are quite narrow and wide outside margins. That makes for gorgeous white space.

But from a practical point of view, the printed book with a hefty page count, may be difficult to read. To read the text in the middle of a thick book with narrow inside margins, you may have to push down the text pages, and in the process, break the spine. Consider the final page count when planning page margins. In this case it makes sense to make the inside and outside margins equal.

There are two more considerations though. If the outside margins are not wide enough, the text appears too close to the page trim. There is no set rule for outside margins.

The solution is to test, creating several pages with different margins and filling the pages with placeholder text. Most importantly, print out the pages. Do not overlook trimming the page to size. Put a half point (0.5-point) rectangle on the page dimensions to use as a trim guide to see on the page printed out, or use the crop marks. You may be surprised at how trimming the page will change the look.

Either allow an image to bleed, or give it a substantial margin. Avoid the mistake of having an image that is only a quarter inch from the trim. This is an example of a page that might look good on the computer screen. But, when printed full size on press and trimmed to size, the mistake of having an image too close to the trim is apparent.

"Safe" margins

Print-on-demand services ask that "safe" margins are used. There is no need for high-quality book printers to require safe margins, as book printing is done on commercial printing presses and in signatures.

POD services are usually outputting a page or two at a time from a digital output device. It is high-end equipment made by copier manufacturers and does what desktop copiers do. They need the safe margin because paper sometimes jostles around when outputting pages.

Also, POD services need to make sure they have enough margin for side-sewn hardcovers. Professionally printed books are never side-sewn. They are printed on press in signatures and professionally bound.

The two-page spread

A spread is one or more images grouped together that are the width of two pages. It crosses over the gutter of the book. There are many self-publishers who come to our company to print books having "printed" a book at a POD service. They often want assurance that two-page spread images will not be clipped off or lost in the gutter, having had this happen before.

This clipping will not happen on the books we print on press and here is why. When pages are output a page or two at a time at a POD service, the entire stack of output pre-trimmed pages is bound together by side-sewing. Books often have two-page spreads. The center of the spread image gets clipped off in the gutter at a POD service. It happens when a book is side-sewn or glued, so that some of the image is simply not seen.

This loss of part of the two-page spread image will never happen when books are printed on press in signatures. The size of the signature depends on the number of pages as well as the size of the sheet. Star Print Brokers always prints on sheet-fed presses, never on web presses using roll stock, and never using digital output.

The signature sheet may have for example, six pages on one side of the sheet and six pages on the other side to make up a 12-page signature. The printed sheet is folded down to the signature size, like a booklet. The booklet-like signatures are then "married" together to form the text block of the book. The printing process is the same for a hardcover book or a soft cover book.

If the book must be print-on-demand, then design the book without any two-page spreads crossing over the gutter. If you do not do this, spreads will be clipped in the middle as shown in this photo of a dog.

Top: No clipping on this two-page spread printed in a signature on a commercial printing press.

Lower: Clipping of a two-page spread digitally output in two single pages. Some of the image is lost in the gutter.

Photo by Victor Grabarczyk on Unsplash

Book page layout

There is a vast amount of information that has been published over the years about book layout. I am distilling the subject down to useful "simple & professional" information, but continue to expand your knowledge. It is said that rules are made to be broken and that is true. However, valuable lessons are learned from years of practical experience.

"Normal" view showing bleeds, margins and columns. The part of the image that bleeds is indicated. This is a single right-hand page which is why the gutter bleed is set to 0 inches.

Toggle to "Preview" to see the page. as it would be trimmed.

Start with a single page and a two-page spread for a coffee table book layout. Later, create master pages and transfer elements to create Paragraph Styles, Character Styles, Swatches, and Object Styles.

Additional information on books other than coffee table books is covered in Chapter 4, *Getting Started* on pages 83 to 89. Master pages are covered in Chapter 5, *Interior Pages*, pages 95 to 96.

GET READY TO TOGGLE

The Toolbox is located on the left side when InDesign is open. Right click on the last icon which is the View Tool. The views to choose from are Normal, Preview, Bleed, Slug, and Presentation.

I am constantly toggling between Normal and Preview when designing books.

Make sure that if an image is to bleed, page bleeds are added to the document. Go to File > Document Set-up. A bleed extends not just to the end of the page, but into the bleed area. The page size does not change. After printing, the area that bleeds is trimmed off.

FIND INSPIRATION

The subject matter of the book may be all the inspiration needed, especially if the book designer is showcasing an artist or a photographer's work. Art and photographs should stand on their own. Body text is set so the type is small, simple, and utilizes lots of white space. Never bleed art images or photographs unless the artist or photographer advises you of their preference to do so, as for specific pages or spreads that bleed on all sides. They generally do not want their art or photography to be trimmed in any way.

Designers have a lot more leeway when it comes to other types of coffee table books. Perhaps they are designing a book about a city or town, the history of anything, or a collection of some sort. Is the book meant to be scholarly, fanciful, or something in between? This makes a difference in how to approach the design.

A designer can select an image provided to them and use it as a theme. It may show up as line art, a badge, scaled to different sizes, in color, in black and white, screened, framed—the list goes on. Design the effect!

In a book I designed about mead, which is made from honey, I used a little bit of honeycomb line art that was screened back and in color. Use this type of effect sparingly, as it should add interest and not overwhelm.

In *Book Design: Simple & Professional*, distinct spreads are used, setting off the parts of the book: Plan, Design, Print, and Sell. A simple color was used and then texture added to it. This did not work. I looked around for another less boring and more inspired solution, always keeping in check my tendency to over design.

A client usually provides graphics or images to draw from for inspiration. Cheap, junky clip art is never used. Also, many clip art services charge an extended royalty fee which is as much as $50 per image or more. While I created the illustrative elements in this book, the overall design needed more. This book is not about how to use Adobe InDesign. A book such as that would require very simple design. But a book about how to design any book needs more design substance.

I am not an illustrator myself, so I bought a collection of Japan-themed graphics from DesignCuts.com. The creator does not charge a royalty for either personal or commercial use. There are quite a few icons, symbols, and textures available that I did not use. Instead, I employed the same color palette throughout, and a feeling of the Japanese esthetic. I did not want the book to look like it was specifically about designing Japanese books!

There are other styled graphics in the package that are being worked into other books as part of my *Simple & Professional* series.

Photographs are on the opening spread for each chapter. They all came from Unsplashed.com and are royalty free. The photographers are all given credit—*thank you*—but it is not required under the current Unsplash rules. I would always rather opt to use original art illustration, or photographs that are not sold commercially.

When picking out photographs to use for a book or any project, make sure to select those with a similar color and value, especially if they are to appear on the same or adjacent pages. Use of any element should blend well with the rest of the book. It is quite permissible to tone images in Photoshop, to have similar color.

Look to other books for inspiration. Something may catch your attention and inspire you to use it in your book. There is nothing wrong with adopting a similar color scheme or using the same typefaces. Perhaps you love the book's dimensions and margins. Maybe you go crazy for the light blue cloth cover wrap with gloss black foil stamping. Never use someone else's art without permission, and never plagiarize. That is theft, not inspiration.

Be sure to give credit next to images from sources other than yourself or the author. Credit might be cited in the copyright text, a footnote, or in acknowledgements. If you have questions about when and how to give credit, use *The Chicago Manual of Style* book or website. The book is an essential asset in any book designer's library.

FUNCTION FIRST

Plan one basic master page first, and then duplicate and modify it as needed for a few basic set-ups. The layout for a coffee table book is much the same as a photography book, or an art book. Do not get too complicated as less is usually more.

You can work in inches, millimeters, or picas. We will not add all means of measuring here, but your changes can be made by going to File > Preferences > and selecting Units and Increments. This is important to know as when Star Print Brokers provides spine width or cover wrap measurements, it is in millimeters, so if I am working in inches or picas, I change over to millimeters for cover wrap, spines, and dust jackets.

Open Document Set-up. Make sure that the "Facing Pages" box is checked. That way, page one will be a right-hand page as it always is in a book. All books have an even number of pages. Every leaf has two sides. If you end up with an odd number, add a page. The "Bleed and Slug" area is below "Margins." You may need to click on the down arrow to see it. A 0.125 inch, 3 mm, or 0p9 pica bleed is added to Top, Bottom, and Outside.

It is permissible to start a chapter on either a right or left-hand page. My preference is to start chapters on a right-hand page, but if you are watching page count closely, you can start a new chapter wherever the previous chapter ends. Remember the first chapter must always begin on a right-hand page.

THE BASIC SINGLE PAGE

Book design is all about creating a style using basic principles and paying attention to page layout. See Chapter 1, *Design Fundamentals*.

When designing a single page, typefaces are determined as are their sizes, body text width, column and gutter widths, page margins, headers or footers, page numbers, captions and credits, and color scheme.

Once satisfied, create the master page using page margins, columns, page numbers, and header or footer placement. You are not wedded to the design. The beauty of creating Masters and Styles is that you can change them globally. Documents in a book can be synchronized so each document does not have to be changed manually. It saves so much time, and books always take longer to complete than you think they will.

THE TWO-PAGE SPREAD

A spread can be set-up like the beginning chapter spreads in this book. Left and right pages that are designed differently from each other. If designing a novel, each spread will have the same format.

I use spreads most often for chapters. This book is a good example. See the footers. The left-hand page remains the same for much of the book. It simply contains the page number and book title. The right-hand page has the chapter name and the page number. I created a new master for each chapter. In addition, there is the two-page spread for the beginning of each chapter. Since some pages are supposed to have no footers, headers or page numbers, a blank page Master is added with only the margins set.

Cover considerations

The cover does not have to match the design style of the book interior. Authors usually write the manuscript in Microsoft Word. The designer then uses the Word document to create a book set-up in Adobe InDesign.

The cover may be created by the same designer, or someone who specializes in cover design. The cost for a cover ranges from $50 to thousands.

Keeping covers simple

A hardcover book has a front cover, back cover, and spine. Dust jackets have flaps. We will go over set-ups for covers and binding style set-ups in Chapter 6, *Cover Design and Binding*. But for now, we will examine the elements that go into a *successful* cover.

While I have many years of experience designing books and book covers, I fall back on the simple principles I learned years ago to design advertisements that sell products and services. Books are similar. Successful is the operative word. Marketing and exposure are vital to book sales, but success starts with great cover design.

FRONT COVER

Book title

The title is the most important element on the cover. Go big or go home! Consider the size of the title's typeface. Once the cover and title are reduced to a thumbnail on Amazon, a book can easily be passed over by potential book buyers. A small title is hard to read on a thumbnail.

The typeface for the title on the cover sets the tone for the book. While I reccommend classic typefaces for the body text from Adobe Fonts, you can use something else that is unique for a title. A one-off typeface from providers like DesignCuts.com may work well. However, make sure that you do not have to pay a royalty unless you are willing to pay for the typeface. Experiment with optical and metric kerning, and letterspacing.

I like big titles because they can be more readily seen in the small thumbnails on Amazon that shoppers see. This is particularly important for use on a portrait-oriented book versus a landscape-orientation. Condensed typefaces work well. Because they are condensed, the type size can be larger than with a non-condensed typeface. The same rules apply to the cover as to the book interior.

The design of the cover can be completely different than the interior, but limit typefaces to two. Three can be used if using a novelty or script typeface. Keep it simple, use white space effectively, and line up text on an imaginary or background grid.

Subtitle

While the subtitle is a secondary consideration, it could mean a lot to the sale of a book. If the title is non-specific or does not convey what the book is about, a subtitle is necessary. Think in terms of feature/benefit statements when writing subtitles. If the title is the feature, then what benefit does the book buyer derive from the feature? At the very least, the subtitle needs to deliver a qualifying statement.

The name of this book is *Book Design: Simple & Professional*. The subtitle adds important information not contained in the title; "For self-publishers and graphic artists using Adobe InDesign." This subtitle qualifies the book title for the book buyer. It helps them to make their buying decision.

Author's name

The author's name should appear on the front cover. Since there may be other book titles that are similar, it is important to have the author's name on the cover in case they ask for or search for the book online. Usually, it goes on the bottom of the cover and the size of the type is up to the designer or the author's preference.

If the author is well-known, a book designer may want to bring the name up higher and make it larger. Afterall, a known author or personality is a selling point.

Graphic elements

Will a photograph, illustration or graphic element be used? What works in the design? What are you trying to convey on the cover? Try making several cover designs from which to choose.

BACK COVER

Sales message

The back cover is where a sales message belongs. Consider using a feature/benefit statement or a short paragraph about the book. Use a larger type size for such paragraphs; a minimum of 14-point or more. Adjust type size in accordance with the number of characters on a line to make the line length comfortable to read. See Chapter 1, *Design Fundamentals*, page 18. If the statement becomes too large because of the number of characters on a line, consider using a condensed type as one of your two typefaces.

Author photo and biography

This is optional. While a biography is something to be included in a book, it can be on a flap of a dust jacket or a French flap of a soft cover book. A photo of the author may be used on the back cover, or another image or two that reflect the content of the book. If an author photo is used, add a short biography in smaller type.

Quotes or testimonials

Sending out copies of the books to be read by respected people or authors may be a great way to get a few of their quotes for the back cover. This is also optional.

What you will find inside

Hitting the high points of the book's content is yet another option. I added the four parts of this book and names of the chapters to interest the targeted book buyer.

Barcode with ISBN

An EAN Bookland barcode is a special kind of barcode and it is mandatory. It is meant specifically for books, and the information it contains is available to all bookstores and on-line retailers.

Unfortunately, when some on-demand providers or even small publishers tout distribution, sometimes, all they are offering is an ISBN. Never accept an ISBN from another party, as they become the publisher of your book. Why accept just royalties when you can retain all profits and all rights?

The only time you might not want to use an ISBN and EAN Bookland barcode is if your book will be sold exclusively in a place that is not a bookstore. Star Print Brokers can sell one ISBN and one barcode as we are authorized agents of ISBN. However, if you are doing more than one format, like a soft cover and an ebook, you will need two ISBNs. It is most cost effective to go directly to isbn.org and buy a pack of ten numbers, as well as one barcode. Ebooks do not use barcodes, but do need an ISBN.

It is customary and most helpful for bookstores to place the barcode in the lower right corner of the back cover. Make sure it is not in the hinge area of the cover.

The barcode needs to be on a white or a very light background, so as not to interfere with scanning. Check with your provider or ISBN for questions about color backgrounds.

When buying a barcode, it may be placed at full size: 100 percent. It is standard to reduce it to 92 percent, and it may be reduced to as small as 80 percent of full size.

SPINE

Positioning

If a book is standing up on a bookshelf as in a library or bookstore, you would tilt your head to your right to read the spine. There are other countries where it is the opposite. The title is placed at the top. The author name is listed next. Sometimes the publishing company has a logo or name on the spine too at the bottom of the spine.

FLAPS

Dust jackets and French flaps

A soft cover book may have one or two flaps that are extensions of the cover. It is evident on this book. The flaps might not have any typesetting or graphics, or maybe just a continuation of background color from the front and back covers. They are a great place to add the author photo and biography on one flap—and a summary of the book on another flap—just as you would see on dust jacket flaps.

Manuscript and captions

It is important to note that a novel can easily be flowed into a pre-made Word template. Unless it is a more complicated layout, Word will suffice. But most other books need to be set-up in InDesign. It is the industry standard.

WRITING THE MANUSCRIPT

If writing the manuscript, the easiest thing to do is to start with a free Microsoft Word template specifically set-up for a book manuscript. Open Word on your device, click "New" in the left column. Type "manuscript" in the search line. A Book Manuscript appears that may be downloaded for free.

When writing, there may be a need to place images. Since images should not be embedded in the InDesign file for printing, add only the name of the image in the manuscript, and not the image itself. Captions and credits may be added along with the name of the photo, or they may be set up on a separate file. But there must be some sort of indication as to where the photos and captions are to go.

This is a good time to make a note for the designer about a full page with bleed or any other instruction. It is up to the author to provide photographs or illustrations that are the correct size. The author needs to verify that the dimensions and resolution are correct for the space they will occupy. See the following pages in this chapter for more on dimensions and resolution.

If the author does not supply the image size required or larger, it is standard that the extra time involved for the designer be charged to the author at the designer's hourly rate. It is an extra charge and falls under Author's Corrections, also known as Author's Alternations, (ACs or AAs). Designers should have this and the hourly rate clearly stated on their quote.

PLACING THE WORD MANUSCRIPT IN INDESIGN

It is assumed that a Basic Paragraph is created in InDesign. Use the "Place" command instead of copying and pasting. This will preserve the format of the text, such as italics. Autoflow the document from page to page. Since this is not a book about InDesign, if you are unsure of how to do this, see Adobe InDesign Help.

DESIGNING CAPTIONS

Captions can be the size of the text, or most often smaller. They may also be in all bold uppercase letters, or in a small-size delicate lowercase font. Be careful not to apply a process color to delicate caption fonts. You might have to change the color on proof. The dot pattern of the rosette may become apparent, especially if they are set in a medium to light color.

Most often, captions are in blacK, made from CMYK. They can also be a tint of black; not less than 50 percent, or another solid spot color. Just remember that if you add a spot ink to a process color job, it adds another ink tray on press and increases the cost of printing.

If using heavy block fonts, this is usually not a problem, but check for this on a physical proof, either digitally output or on a press proof.

Collecting photos and images

Copy and store images and photographs in an art or asset folder that is in a separate folder, preserving originals.

Many of the images used in this book, including the cover, are from Unsplash.com. They are free. Unsplash states in the licensing agreement in place at the time of the writing of this book that the photos may be credited or not, and that they are free for commercial use. If you are interested in using Unsplash, please refer to their licensing agreement at: https://unsplash.com/license

Read licensing agreements for all images and graphics used. There are costs associated with many stock images on stock photo or clip art websites, as well as restricted use on the number impressions that may be published in different media. Some offer extended use agreements at a higher cost.

Photographs that you purchase, acquire for free, or that you shoot yourself need to be converted to CMYK in Adobe® Photoshop® to print well on press. They must also be TIFs or JPGs. Do not use PNGs as they are for the web and not for book printing. Star Print Brokers can convert photos or images as part of the book design process, at an additional cost.

When collecting photographs from several sources, realize that each photo may have a quite different look. This may be problematic in having a unified look. Start with similar looking images whenever possible.

Solutions:

- Use images with the same hue or value from one artist or one photographer.
- Adjust the color in photos so that they are all toned the same way.
- Use a color overlay or ghost the images.
- Buy Photoshop overlays that provide a similar look for each image, like an antique look, bright, light airy photos, or a dark and moody overlay, etc.

Color in photographs and images

The color viewed on a monitor may look different vs. the same color viewed on a different monitor. Unless you have a color-calibrated monitor and are sitting in a color booth, precise matching proof color might not be possible. This is true of a physical, digitally output proof or a press proof. However, the color is much better on newer computers than it was in years past.

Color houses in the 1990s and before, used the terms "pleasing color" and "exact match."

PLEASING COLOR

When Star Print Brokers supplies a physical set of full-color proofs, the entire set is output from a digital output device. This is our standard proof, but not necessarily the standard elsewhere. The color is close to what will be printed on press, but approximates the printed book. We still use the term "pleasing color."

EXACT MATCH COLOR

Press proofs or wet proofs are printed on press, ink on paper. This option is quite costly. Seldom is there a necessity for exact match proofs. Besides, our digital proofs are most often so close in color that exact match is not required. We try to achieve an "exact match" using press proofs or wet proofs.

Occasionally we work with a photographer or an artist who has an exceptionally keen eye for color. While we can please ninety-nine percent of the self-publishers, we cannot guarantee that every page of every individual book will have the exact same match as on the printed press proof.

However, Star Print Brokers reputation since 1999 is that we produce exquisite color reproduction. *Printing is an art, not a science.*

Resolution for book printing

There are a couple of rules to follow for the optimum resolution necessary to print images without them looking pixilated in print. Read below about size and resolution.

SIZE

Always use photographs or images at the dimensions they will be when printed, or larger. Keep in mind the dimensions of the image when it is enlarged or reduced, and then placed in the document. Save as TIFs or JPGs.

RESOLUTION

The resolution must be 300 ppi or larger. What matters is the effective resolution. To view in InDesign., go to Links. Highlight an image. In the panel below the links, see the Effective PPI as well as the Actual PPI.

An image with an Actual PPI of only 72 for example may print at an acceptable effective resolution if the dimensions are quite large. That is because the image can be *reduced*, so that the Effective PPI *increases*.

Simply put, reducing an image with a low Actual PPI means that you are increasing the Effective PPI.

BEWARE OF "REZING UP"

Do not increase resolution artificially, even if you see that you are allowed to do in Photoshop. This is called rezing up.

There is no substitution for the original digital or scanned image. If the image is rezed up, the printed image will be pixilated, *even if it looks fine on your monitor*. That is because images can be viewed on monitors at only 72 ppi or 92 ppi instead of the 300 ppi required for print.

The solution is to recreate the image, rescan the original image, or buy a larger image.

DESTINATION SPACE

Check with your printer. Star Print Brokers uses U.S. Sheetfed Coated v2 when printing on coated stock. In Photoshop, go to File > Convert to Profile. Select Profile: U.S. Sheetfed Coated v2.

Creating new images

When creating new images in Photoshop, make sure they will print well on press. If you simply need to convert existing images, skip this section, and go on to "Converting existing images from RGB to CMYK."

Open Photoshop and then open a new document. Go to File > New . . . See the Preset Details on the right side of the open window as replicated in the illustration above. Save as TIFs or JPGs.

WIDTH AND HEIGHT

Set width and height to a minimum of the size they will be when printed in the book. Larger is okay. So many designers and illustrators seem to miss the importance of this. The dimensions of an image are just as important as the resolution. If you are creating many of the same types of images such as screen shots, follow the same sizing for each image. All images should be of the same type to be consistent.

RESOLUTION
300 Pixels/Inch (or more).

COLOR MODE
CMYK Color

BACKGROUND CONTENTS
Select the option that works best for the image you are creating, usually **white or transparent**.

ADVANCED OPTIONS > COLOR PROFILE
Select **U.S. Sheetfed Coated v2**, unless using uncoated stock. Verify the color profile with your printer.

Select **Create** and **Save** the image, preferably as a tif or as a jpg.

Convert existing images from RGB to CMYK

Check with your printer before you convert images as they may have a particular color profile they use. Star Print Brokers prints books on offset sheetfed presses. They use U.S. Sheetfed Coated v2 for most books.

If books are printed on uncoated or woodfree stock, they use **U.S. Sheetfed Uncoated v2.** "SWOP" is never used as we do not print on web presses. To convert images in Photoshop, go to **Edit > Convert to Profile**, and make your selection from the pull-down menu.

COLOR SHIFT

There may be a shift in color when any photo or image is converted from RGB to CMYK. Most often, it appears in blues such as in skies or in hot pink or fuchsia. Photographs with metal colors may also change too. Blues and pinkish watercolor images will likely shift in color. The shifts occur because CMYK has a more limited color array than RGB.

Batch conversion is not recommended. It is important that the client see any shift in color between the original and converted images.

Actual and effective resolution

Effective resolution is sometimes puzzling to self-publishers and designers. Book printing requires resolution at 300 ppi or larger, *and* the photograph or image needs to be at the size it will be when printed. This is where effective resolution comes into play.

- **Actual resolution** is the resolution of a photograph or image at 100%.
- **Effective resolution** is the resolution after the image is enlarged or reduced. The effective resolution is what counts.

Images for the web

RESOLUTION: 72 to 96 ppi

COLOR MODE: RGB

FORMAT: JPG or PNG

Images for Book Printing

Book printing uses a resolution of 300 ppi in a JPG or TIF format. They must be at the size they will be when printed in the book, or larger.

RESOLUTION: 300 ppi

COLOR MODE: CMYK or other Pantone libraries.

    Example: Pantone + Color Bridge Coated for coated stock.

    Example: Pantone + Color Bridge Uncoated for uncoated stock.

    Example: CMYK if you are picking a color out of a photograph with the eyedropper tool.

FORMAT: JPG or TIF

EXAMPLE OF ADJUSTING FOR EFFECTIVE RESOLUTION

Let's suppose that all your photos are 72 ppi, but they are a whopping 32 inches wide. This is where a little bit of math comes in, or just place the image in InDesign. Go to Links and highlight an image.

Watch the Effective Resolution *increase* as you *reduce the image* to the page width, or smaller.

There is no substitution for the original scan or a high-resolution photo. A low-res image may look sharp on your monitor, because everything looks good on a monitor that only needs 72 ppi. However, this low-resolution image will not print well. It will be pixelated.

Author and designer responsibilities

I am not an attorney, so the following are just suggestions based on my exper-ience. When it comes to copyrights, permissions, contracts, legal entities, etc., get legal advice.

Author responsibilities and suggestions

- Obtain permissions to use images, quotes, or any material not created by the author. Keep a record of permissions.
- Provide an edited Microsoft Word document to the designer. Include text for the copyright page, table of contents, index, and glossary, if applicable.
- Images are provided by the author. Indicate placement in manuscript. Image captions and credits may be provided in a separate document.
- Choose the printer or service and provide book dimensions and binding style to the designer. Spine width is determined after final page count.
- The author or designer may convert images to CMYK. Verify the correct format with the service. Color may shift when converting from RGB.
- Indicate approximate image sizes. *Example:* Note full pages with bleeds. Images must be 300 ppi or larger, and at the approximate size or larger when printed. Designers have more flexibility if given 350 ppi images.
- Buy an ISBN and barcode to be provided to the designer.
- Pay a deposit with the balance due on completion. I charge 50 percent.
- The author pays for any graphics or images that are purchased with their permission and on their behalf.
- Additional hourly design time is charged to the author as Author's Corrections (ACs), also called Author's Alterations (AAs).
- Write in Microsoft Word. Design and formatting should be in InDesign.

HOW MANY PAGES IS 50,000 WORDS?

The question can be answered if the typeface, point size, leading, page size, and margins are known. A provider who prints novels with the same dimensions and specifications, can provide page count based on the manuscript. For any other book type, it is just a guess.

Book designer responsibilities and suggestions

- Do not layout a book until all permissions are provided.
- Provide two or three text layout and cover ideas. They can be sketches or

just a typeset page or two of a couple of ideas to get started. Charge for additional unexpected preliminary work.

- Provide a written estimate of design fees. Detail everything to avoid misunderstandings. Include hourly rates or any agreement for additional work or corrections. Collect a deposit and the signed contract after sample design work is approved.
- Consider using a professional design contract, like forms found in the *Graphic Artists Guild Handbook, Pricing & Ethical Guidelines*.
- The author or designer may convert images to CMYK. Verify the correct format with the printer. Color may shift when converting to CMYK.
- Never change the author's manuscript without permission. Make changes for book design and typography. *Example:* Use one space between sentences instead of two, correct use of hyphens, en and em dashes, etc.
- Send PDFs proofs regularly.
- Provide print-ready PDFs once the book design is completed.
- It is customary *not* to provide the final InDesign documents to the author, but many designers do provide them.

HOW LONG DOES IT TAKE TO DESIGN A BOOK?

If my desk is clear, I finish the design and layout of a 180- to 200-page book of average difficulty, in two to three weeks, assuming all materials are provided with a deposit and signed contract. Add extra time to design a few sample pages before you proceed. Complicated books such as cookbooks or books with charts will take more time. High page count books will naturally add to the timeline. New or inexperienced book designers should allow more time. If a designer plans to design books on evenings and weekends, the timeline should be increased. Always provide your clients with a realistic timeline. You want return business and word-of-mouth referrals.

WORKING WITH AUTHORS

Book designers and authors may have conflicting design ideas. Try to establish priorities with the author. If the author seems to want everything bolder and bigger, try instead to make other elements smaller and lighter.

Give the client what they want. But take your name off the book if you are not proud of the work. Be flexible to accommodate the author. But, if you know it is poor design, politely decline credit by excluding yourself as the designer on the copyright page.

Divisions in a book
Front matter
Text or body matter
Back matter

BOOK STRUCTURE
Pages and Divisions

ALL BOOKS HAVE DIVISIONS FOR THE INTERIOR. This influences how a book will be compiled. The author takes into consideration the parts of a book for each division. A designer needs to know if the part begins on a right- or left-hand page. Blank pages may be used. For instance, if there are two parts, each one page long and both are right-hand pages to follow each other, a blank page is inserted in between.

The pages of a book printed on press usually print in 8-, 12-, or 16-page signatures. We can print fewer pages in a signature, but it is not half the cost for a lower page count signature.

Example: A manuscript is completed with 108 pages, or 14 8-page signatures; 8 x 14 = 112 pages, so 4 pages available in the signature.

 QUICK TIPS

- The divisions are front matter, text, and back matter.
- Every leaf is two pages because it has a front side and a back side.
- Front matter is numbered in Roman numerals. The text and the back matter is numbered in Arabic numerals.

Divisions in a book

The divisions in a book consist of front matter, text, and back matter. First, we need to describe what a page is versus a leaf.

A *page* in a book is one side of a *leaf*. A leaf has a front and a back side; *recto* and *verso*. If you have a 100-page book, that means the leaf count is 50. When requesting a quote for printing or design, the page count is 100. Sometimes people provide an odd number, like 99. We wonder if the person means 99 leaves or 198 pages. The page count is always an even number. The number of leaves is irrelevant. Blank pages count.
- *Recto* is a right-hand page and the first to be read.
- *Verso* is a left-hand page, read second.

Photo by Christian Perner on Unsplash

The following chart is used with the permission of *The Chicago Manual of Style*:

FRONT MATTER

Half title page	i
Series title, frontispiece, or blank	ii
Title page	iii
Copyright page	iv
Dedication	v
(Table of) Contents	v or vi
(List of) Illustrations	recto or verso
(List of) Tables	recto or verso
Foreword	recto
Preface	recto
Acknowledgments (if not part of preface)	recto or verso
Introduction (if not in back matter)	recto
Abbreviations (if not in back matter)	recto
Chronology (if not in back matter)	recto
Second half title	recto

TEXT

First text page (introduction or chapter 1) or	1
Second half title or first part title	1
Blank	2
First text page	3

BACK MATTER

Acknowledgments (if not in front matter)	recto
Appendix (or first, if more than one)	recto
Second and subsequent appendices	recto or verso
Chronology (if not in front matter)	recto
Abbreviations (if not in front matter)	recto
Notes	recto
Glossary	recto
Bibliography or References	recto
(List of) Contributors	recto
Illustration Credits (if not in captions or elsewhere)	recto
Index(es)	recto

Front matter

There are some mandatory pages in front matter. *Book Design: Simple & Professional* is designed with notes in light gray type at the bottom of specific pages. Optional pages are noted along with whether they are a right- or left-hand page. Some can be either. See the chart preceding this page.

- **Half title page** (optional). If used, it is page *i*. Depending on the number of pages needed to print a signature, you may use the half title page to adjust page count.
- **Series title, frontispiece, or blank** is next, on page *ii*.
- **Title page** is page *iii*, or it is page *i*, if a half title page is not used.
- **Copyright page**, a left-hand page, following title page. List the country where the book is printed. Use the name of the person or the entity that holds the copyright. Consult an attorney with any questions. *Example:* © 2021 by [author name or entity]. All rights reserved.
- **Dedication** may follow (optional), and it is a right-hand page.
- **Table (of contents)** is next and may start on a right- or left-hand page. Contents may be on one page or several pages.
- **(List of) Illustrations** may start on a right- or left-hand page.
- **(List of) Tables** may start on a right- or left-hand page.
- **Foreword** (optional) follows, starting on a right-hand page. It is written by someone other than the author.
- **Preface** (optional) is next, starting on a right-hand page. The author writes the preface.
- **Acknowledgments** (optional) follows the preface, starting on a right-hand page. It may instead appear in the back matter.
- **Introduction** (optional) or may be in back matter. The Introduction may start on a right- or left-hand page.
- **Abbreviations** (optional) or may be in back matter, and they start on a right-hand page.
- **Chronology** (optional) in front matter or may be in back matter, starting on a right-hand page.
- **Second half title** (optional) and is a right-hand page.
- Lowercase Roman numerals are used in the front matter. The first page of a book is page 1, or i, and is always a right-hand page.
- Many front matter page numbers are *not* visible. Instructions for page number set-up on masters, and the use of masters, paragraph styles, and character styles in Chapter 5, *Interior Pages* on pages 95 to 99.

BASIC PAGES

FRONT matter
(optional = gray)

Text or body matter

All text between the front matter and the back matter is the body matter or text of the book. The first page following front matter is the first page of a chapter, part, or section; whatever the author includes in the book.

- The front matter begins with page *i* and the body matter begins with page 1, always a right-hand page. When requesting a printing quote, add the page count of the front matter to the page count of the body matter and back matter. Blanks do count.
- The body matter is numbered in Arabic numerals.

Back matter

Not every book has back matter. For instance, a novel seldom has need for back matter.

- **Acknowledgments** (if not in front matter) is optional and starts on a right-hand page.
- **Appendix** (or first, if more than one) is optional, and starts on a right-hand page.
- **Second and subsequent appendices** (optional) and may start on a right- or left-hand page.
- **Chronology** (optional) and (if not in front matter) starts on a right-hand page.
- **Abbreviations** is optional, and, if not in front matter, starts on a right-hand page.
- **Notes** (optional) starts on a right-hand page.
- **Glossary** (optional) and the glossary always starts on a right-hand page.
- **Bibliography or References** (optional) Each of these start on a right-hand page.
- **(List of) Contributors** (optional) starts on a right-hand page.
- **(List of) Illustration Credits** (if not in captions or elsewhere) starts on a right-hand page and is optional.
- **Index(es)** is optional and starts on a right-hand page.
- The back matter is numbered with Arabic numerals.

BODY matter
(optional = gray)

70   BOOK DESIGN: SIMPLE & PROFESSIONAL

ADVANCED PAGES

FRONT matter (optional = gray)

	Half title / i
blank / ii	Title page / iii
Copyright / iv	Dedication / v
blank or Contents / vi	Contents / vii
Illustrations / viii	Tables / ix
Tables cont'd or blank / x	Foreword / xi
Foreword cont'd or blank / xii	Preface / xiii

Preface cont'd, blank or Acknowledgments / xiv	Acknowledgments or Introduction / xv
Introduction cont'd or blank / xiv	Abbreviations / xv
blank / xiv	Chronology / xv
blank / xiv	Second half title / xv
blank / xiv	

BODY matter (optional = gray)

	First text page (introduction or chapter 1) or Second half title or first part title / 1
blank / 2	First text page / 3

BACK matter (optional = gray)

	Acknowledgments / cont'd from body / Arabic numeral
blank / Arabic numeral	Appendix / Arabic numeral
Appendix cont'd or blank / Arabic numeral	Second appendix may start on right or left / Arabic numeral
Second appendix cont'd or blank / Arabic numeral	Chronology / Arabic numeral
Chronology cont'd or blank / Arabic numeral	Notes / Arabic numeral
Notes cont'd or blank / Arabic numeral	Glossary / Arabic numeral
Glossary cont'd or blank / Arabic numeral	Bibliography or References / Arabic numeral

Bibliography or References cont'd or blank / Arabic numeral	(List of) Contributors / Arabic numeral
(List of) Contributors cont'd or blank / Arabic numeral	(List of) Illustration Credits / Arabic numeral
(List of) Illustration Credits cont'd or blank / Arabic numeral	Index(es) / Arabic numeral
Index(es) cont'd or blank / Arabic numeral	

CHAPTER THREE | BOOK STRUCTURE   71

PART TWO

Design

The Grid System and Big Picture

Creating a grid in InDesign

White space

InDesign files needed by book binding

Coffee table books

Cookbooks

Novels

Photography and art books

Picture books

Board books

Reference books

GETTING STARTED
Types of Books

By now you have most of the basic information, even if you are new to book design. In this chapter, tweak InDesign, read about the Grid System, white space, and the InDesign files needed by book binding type, as well as the special features of different types of books.

 QUICK TIPS

- Understand grids whether you use them or not. However, always consider the use of alignment.
- White space is invaluable. Do not fill up every last bit of a page.
- Different book files are needed according to binding type and possible options.
- Print out, trim, and view some pages before sending PDFs to press.

The Grid System and Big Picture

An underlying structure behind the type and images on a page layout is a grid. It is limiting in that you cannot place images and type anywhere you like. That is also the benefit.

The "Big Picture" style is another standard way to design, and with good reason, especially with some book styles. Who wants a photography book with tiny thumbnail images?

Neither style is mandatory, but both may be helpful in book design. Placement of margins, type, and images are not random. There is a structure to follow to have unity in form and function.

The Grid and Swiss style

The International Style is also known as Swiss Style. There are traditionally specific fonts and colors used in Swiss Style Design. It is a distinctive style that has its roots in the 1920s and '30s and was further developed in Switzerland.

Photo by Hugo Barbosa on Unsplash

The influence of Swiss Design was prevalent throughout the 1950s and is still seen as a design style today.

The Grids used in Swiss design can be a tool in page design and unifies the composition in a rational way. However, it is only a framework and does not solve all design problems. A grid is all about the page layout, margins, and space between columns. It is consistent typographic elements arranged to present a unifying layout.

Designing a book can be easier once the grid and stylesheets are established and implemented. Some designers feel it is too constricting, but once you start to work with a grid, it does solve problems. A grid is used to define the page layout in a logical arrangement of columns, type, and images. Be clear with use of titles, headlines, subtitles, captions, and the arrangement of images and photographs.

A book should be easy to follow and clear to read. A coffee table book should be especially interesting and pleasing to read or thumb through. Is it necessary to use a grid? No, but a novel for instance, will look more professional with an underlying grid. Understand what the grid system is, whether you use it or not. Always use alignment in page layout.

The grid system is easy to imitate, but for a new self-publisher, it can be daunting because there are go many possibilities and ways to structure a grid on a page. While you may have several versions of a basic page, be consistent and logical, arranging elements to maintain consistency throughout the book design.

There is much that is written about grid systems. The goal of this book is to offer valuable information about book design that is simple and professional. There are a number of books that have been written about grid systems if you want to explore this topic in more detail.

Big Picture

The Big Picture style is clean and uses white space effectively. It is a desired style for large format books. The idea in designing an art book, photography book, and most coffee table books is to display large images. Readers are attracted to big pictures. A prominent headline should be incorporated into the layout, with smaller body text.

When designing a large format book, I sometimes fall back on my years of training, designing, and instructing my staff about advertisement design. Some suggestions are intertwined in the following points.

- The top of the ad is the focus. A minimum of 40 to 50 percent of the ad should be the big picture. The idea is to attract the reader's attention so that they read the rest of the copy. Just remember that you only have a few seconds to grab attention and make a favorable impression.
- The headline can be above or below the picture. Depending on the graphic design style, the headline can be large or small, on top or below the picture, or overlay a full-page picture. Coffee table books have fewer headlines of course, but images in a book are usually captioned and credited in small type.
- Even for books, it may be a helpful hint to remember that in advertising, we try to write feature / benefit statements. State the feature followed by the benefit the reader can derive from that feature. This can also be a list of bulleted features and benefits. Okay, not so much for most book content but a valuable tip for back covers and flaps!
- The text copy need not be in large type, as that takes away from the space needed for the big picture. Text should be the same throughout the book unless there is a distinctively different style. It should be 10-, 11-, or at most, 12-point type.
- The back cover of a book might contain a logo and contact information. If so, it belongs toward the bottom of a back cover. Contact information should also always be on the copyright page.

If you had an entire photography or art book with large headlines, it would be overwhelming. Back off on the headline size—except for a specific use—just as at the beginning of a chapter.

Creating a grid in InDesign

Although this book is not teaching InDesign, creating a baseline grid is included as it is helpful in book design, particularly for books with a great deal of body copy.

There are two kinds of grids. They are a baseline grid and a document grid. The baseline grid is to align columns of text and rows of text. The document grid looks like graph paper, having squares. Either grid style can be customized. But when a baseline grid is set up, it will be on every spread. It cannot be assigned to any master.

There are two examples of baseline grids on the following pages. The grid lines in the examples do not match up to the text lines, but are helpful

Uciet porrum num nis dis

Harit alique volendu ciandiora eatiore pelesci utasint vollia solor sequi blant andit et offic tem in nonsecum eostrunt est, serorpo rendem nis ad quia simus sumquam illa non re alicia dolliquiatet maximus preptassi acesequos et, voluptur? Quias et alicitate volorest, sinist, con rerorit illessi millianda verion cumquisci omnit faccum eumquodiscim fugitatur maximet liquia sunt laboreptatum duciis aut eaquas quamus qui nobis quam rat pereser speraturia con pere cum ullore vitem et fuga. Ut dolestrum landi omnist, ut ea vellore rchicim et fugiam res si ullantio. Ga. Ut omnis nus aut minvent et aut eliae nia sumquae placepel modictatur, optas doluptatus sum ut aspit doluptatem doluptatio dollend itassit eum et ditaspient molore, nobitat maxim erorrovidit quati dolo invendit quosant volecul luptasi dolupit aturecea a cuptate plibus est adipsus, optat volorrumque non cus re volupta si ut volorem porrovidi accuptam, sum rem repre, vid modiscimus aborecus, con rerum quisinveres minciis impos voluptat. Acest eum volorep tatus, corepta conetur, omnia quaepud antures editam conse nonse rem. Nequass uscium qui bea nam quia quia cones derovid ent in prae. Et fugiam et, qui ute doluptur alignim inisin nusam ea volupta tionsectia sinvel ma dis ad etur sim dellend icienis molectem voluptatum re ma qui corest ea cusae re velecae sequiduciis iscienti ipietur ad qui restium arum doluptae volupta tecturi acipsam nullaboribus auta nos es quia doluptat plit pratem rectore nis eos rem re sam, iusam, num fuga. Num voluptatem voluptat faccum quam fugias ex esent ant aborunt am dolupti anisin conet occatem quaercia pore nus, eosam coritati doloremped quiate ped minciae nobis etus vel ipit que veliquis aut amuscium rehenim sum utemporent eaquae rem sus alibus poreperor sinulpa ipit volupta quidele nitaspietur, net aliquis enis idempost, sunt laut rendaeperem es repere earcil endi quam, tem lab into blaborem quamus arit que inus ea diate imillore perum apiciis dolest, odit del magnim sumqui as reiumquat mil magnam, ulparum nonseque expliquas idunt, alia voloreh enihillam sinis quid quo blacesciam, que nus maximax imetus sandele cuptaspienti oditibe ruptat unt, volenistrum hici doluptius illis dunt, aut fuga. Sedignat. Fuga. Obitiam alique nissini reptior reri quatiorem ex et prem verrum exceate pa dolenest aut inisquate ate dolupta eptatias resti volorumquid moluptiorio quisciu saepta con ea volum corem qui cuptiate voluptas aliqui volum, quis pla voluptae nos sed quaeper sperorrum quam, cupis dellatiat proreprætio cum que parum adit qui invendior rem.

Um et libersp eliate verferspe nem es dolo te alitate serferi temolup tatiis di aut venihitas estorer ferspic tet ra venimi, solo veria volupic iuntiusa dolupis eictinctate voluptatia doluptum eaquiatin nonsent facidisit harum aliquis rest ero estem as voluptio tem hil molupta tendell oribusc imporrumqui dolum aut ius, te estiunt dia quis ea pelluptatur? Edit pra quamentes am, comnimporro il mossi alit, estet aliam dolles essitatas quam eum qui ius quae non por rerciis dolorem etus dolutes aut ut esto cum is nimporis doluptatin rehenti busam, nullaut aut ventemporro beaqui ut inumquiassim vollesto occab il exerae maximos as et alicili quibea cus ut am audio con et et duscia et quiam evellorrum hit mod ma quatur adisci nem faceaqu ianimus sitisimi, optas et, endebit, quae consenducid maxim et est que nos asim sandaes sunt officiis debitae in conesequas estionsequi to imusdam, inctur minciae de et ditaturem quiae natur, nesendisita del iminimint et ut maxima endam as maionsenient volupta turisse nditati bearis abo. Nequatio. Nam estiat harum culla etur as dendipsa sequiditia acerum faccusdam di consedi dem atur? Sequo mos si a quis est event veres eaquatas ipiene plite volor simagni entionsequos porunte cepudipsam qui quibeaquam sitem endantem inctur? Hillaborro berspe nust eicto ipsamusam, ant mos isquo cus sedicilles dollaborero coreprore et vendignis alibus, con poribus. Fugiti imolora tectas disciis etur audae num reprae. Nobitat emperiosanis doluptat lat eturibus eatiate cus velendundel et asinctusam harumqui ut volut ad molor molut volorrum et dolo eostem atur mint modicius deria de vit arum nit offici dernatus cone reium lacessecto bea quia pliqui sum que suntio. Ut quuntur suntis minus, ommolupturia pratur sed ea sapist aut aut ad quiantus inctate cusda dis everum sitio earis mos est eat lignis ad mossitat et fugitecus dicia eturibeaquam de dit eatempe doloreh enihitas et am, sum quias dolupta tiatur, odit, untures plicieniti dolutes sitio. Equodigent. Exeris alibus et labori nam eatio. Aliquost autempe rehenim et moles apernatur soluptur? It, into endigen dellandelles exeriatum volenectus dolupta volut abo. Itas debis etur a comnis qui oditate vel ium ratinctum nonet lab il is atur, omni dolum que vellabore, qui tessuntus raecatur molent eatiasit, optassim faciissum di quia dolorit exerferum quodi corio est asim harcia qui del eum res sit assit maios ilibus endite si dusdam doluptia consequunte sit ent, solenihilit dolores tiostruntia invelle nestinum quatur? Magname volorep eribeates most harum estiant eum ilitatium

A grid with 8 fields for images and text.

78   BOOK DESIGN: SIMPLE & PROFESSIONAL

Harciam res ium et doloritis sum

Moloreic tem eum fugiti to blanimo luptati berior arumet harum vellabo. Officiemquae nat mo torestiis est, veriberum non num quost pelitendae expla vel int. Cus exerum velitem rempos dolorer isciet utem int reicaborerum ut quas eos dit et aceres consed et et la nis eum rem nihicte molupta tenderferum que nime exerist esequi omniet, arumquatur? Quibus sunt volecea rchiciet aliqui occumquiatem volupta sequi resti tecus assimo conecullaut dust, cum nost cullam suntias esciis de sam, ea adi dolupta prerunt Venis comnis dolest fugiaed tempor sam inci int hitia cus reprovi ticris eatiasit mod que dolut eaquatemodis et verferrovit, qui vendighime nullaccabor aribus nullecto te numqui reperum am, que et estrupt atempor aut ex escite laut quam inciis estrum volorer rorecto modis adit vereper rovidi officid qui tet que verum ad earuntem volum qui que dolupta spient quidunt as apellig enihit aboreiunt as quam nis estibus sinus eos platque cus, ut aut elibus et aborerd ienducid utem dolora ium harum voluptam escipid maionecto quisci te volorernque pa doluptatis et et apiet etur, que ad experum venihil modis aut offic totatem dolorep edignatet a voluptaspe dignat verum utem facerspera sim asint litae peris doluptae nis qui rest, velibus pelis necti od esequam, cum hil et de nectasit qui dolupta cum cone dis et periberiam eumque nihil mollaut lianiscius essimagnam et eicit aut as evel magni omniet prature et et faces si doloressim que cdi solorum et quos sandit ut offictatur ad es pa paritat fugia nos quis molupta quaestis res simod quaectatiate sum fuga. Harit, quae nos minimi voloresto occum sus colorrundis iliciatibust quosa nobis volores aut im cumquis conem et et la prest venda con consequia quam latusapiet quatem et aditat eium aut landit qui tempore ssimus, omnihi igendellest repudae perfere nihillenis modicipsamus as demodis accae volut hiliquo es aut quid quo quodictur aut volut prae veniae re corerit in rest, sitatent dolupis ma aut volorum alit moloria deliquo te dolores sequo expliqui cum everiberio to illa qui omnimpost natent ut omniet, offictectem quo volorem. Officia natet quatum quibusam quae exceperum harum fuga Ebitaep uditati simusda ipsanto magnihicipsa in ero

Eruptatatum hitio et ut mod event lant, sum fugit alibus, cum haribus del eatum a eaque re nonsequi nulluptatquo es evenihici doluptatia non reptatur molorem. Itatess inullit eum et volendit ut dolupti ssimus volupta dolupta eceroresti consequid everis molupta dollibus. Nus corunte veriberupts dent assi con cupturibus as mi, nobitat prae plibus am dis mollorrum exeri intia di dolupta tioremo luptas ut faccabo reribus et ut et autatatias nosant enisimintet explitasit officipid maximpo rporeprate et vent qui ducimagnam, ut audandi ipiducientur autas doleces ut ea pos modis ut maio optatem perum qui alis modignimus vitibus et, quidestibus reicia eos explias ma vitas enisqui simperupient a evenihic to idus endit omnit ut quis et, tem. Nistotas enducipit omnimagnis aut odist aliquist, asimaxim re velesti nim et poreped magnis quaecto ratur, eici destibus et quam aut lam re, si nis porepel iquiatium nus prestorerum verro totae conet quias reiur, con cullum que vendis adi cuptati de expliquatquo molesto eic tem quis vollabor resto blaturit, untur sant aut aborro tet autet la quoditas quunt et lacimol estisti busdam remporibus maximil igent. Ximagniam quatibusam remolore venit, ut voluptatum vel ilitatur, sitem reperum, omnimus, que volupta ad quatisqui accuptat ament. Cias prae sam aut dollore iciaerio qui sime pliquatur a volor arumet venis mint idit fugiatiis ipicti susam dolore, necte velia nihil molorat emporeh enditistia nus, optat repe volless imusdaes cusdae sit perrum fugit landiatis nihicillabo. Adipsam, tem nonsedita sit vercias enis millent urerro millenis eum

Cilit que sitatibust, ab int volupta provitibusa niendit is doluptatquat volla illati is et eum aut aceatiuriat laborumqui ut ut qui quunt ut ulpa doluptis dolupta spicia voles mi, santo quae officiis que corro que sundandanis pre, officiet fuga. Illab ipsaperum dolorum natur mintin ped exeri culpa dem ut aciis rendest fugitatur, tem a quam con et vendellabo. Cat. Genes maximol uptaquunt, simporepelit audanitis mil et elibusandam ut mi, conserunt fuga. Mollab imusdanim aut ommolorum am aut alique

Nam suntius vitati dolo officimodi a dolor restio berum inciur sum videmporit voluptatus, santo mossimo diciderum sit quasinc ipsae. Nam cusam ne dolut asiminis es voluptam quis dolorae comnimpos es sinum, sit ut et lit et eum que quo quiandam, quamusdam estemporro omnis eium, es ut faccuptaes milicia sa voloreculpa volestrupta digendiciam qui optium ad quaspitas ernatem alit, coremped quam volum nisinct orenis expeliqui odia quia pliquatiis delenis ulluptatur, comnis sum esentio repella tqu

A grid with 20 fields for images and text.

in planning columns, white space, and placement of images. They can also be set to have a grid line for every line of type which is different than these example pages.

SETTING THE GRID LINE TO BE THE SAME AS THE TEXT LINE

This text is 11/16, meaning that the text is 11-point and the leading is 16-point. In this example, set the grid to 16-point also. If the pages are complex, using headlines, subheadings, numbered or bulleted text, use half of the leading, or 8-point. I find it helpful to also add a new body text Paragraph Style that is half the leading or 8-point for this document—11/8. This would only be used to add a half line of space.

Remember to toggle between Normal and Preview to view or hide the grid lines.

IMAGES

As a rule, make images the same content size throughout the book. Perhaps a page layout calls for one large image and a column of text. If using the same style on subsequent pages in the book, make sure the image occupies the same size space on each page, and the text column is the same width and type size on each of the same style pages.

Be careful not to come to close the edge of the page. To judge for yourself what is too close, print out the page with trim and bleed marks. It is different seeing the trimmed page versus seeing it on the screen.

White space

It is vital to use white space correctly in page layouts. New designers as well as self-publishers are tempted to fill every little bit of white space on a page and have very skimpy margins. Evaluate other books that may be like yours or have design you admire. Do not copy or plagiarize, but be inspired to create your own page layouts. It is an especially ugly mistake to tighten the leading between lines or enlarge type to fill up a page. This also applies to websites.

Dropping the text point size and allowing wider margins on a page may be just what is needed for effective use of white space. The worst thing you can do is have skinny margins and type that is too large or two lines that are too close together. White space can better display text and images Equally as important: White space is what sells the design!

CHAPTER FOUR | GETTING STARTED   81

InDesign files needed by book binding

Graphic artists are sometimes uncertain how to set-up book binding types in InDesign. The following is a list of the files you will need to create for the most common book binding styles. Also, Wire-O® may be hardcover or soft cover.

InDesign set-ups follow. Most books fall into the following types.

Soft cover book

A book is created to hold chapters, but the .indb book is not submitted. The PDFs to submit are as follows:

- Individual chapter PDFs or entire text
- Cover — front, back, spine PDF (and flaps, if desired)
- Spot varnish PDF (if applicable)
- Emboss or foil PDF (if applicable)

Hardcover with material cover wrap

A book is created to hold chapters, but the .indb book is not submitted. The PDFs to submit are as follows:

- Individual chapter PDFs or entire text PDF
- Blind and / or foil stamp PDF (foil stamp is usual, but it is optional)
- Sticker image for front cover (optional)
- Endpapers PDF (if endpapers are printing)
- Dust jacket PDF (optional)
- Spot varnish PDF (if applicable)

Hardcover with printed cover wrap

A book is created to hold chapters, but the .indb book is not submitted. The PDFs to submit are as follows:

- Individual chapter PDFs or entire text PDF
- Cover wrap PDF to print on press
- Endpapers PDF (if endpapers are printing)
- Dust jacket PDF (optional)
- Spot varnish PDF (if applicable)

See book set-up in Chapter 5, *Interior Pages*. Cover set-ups are found in Chapter 6, *Cover Design & Binding* on pages 107 – 113. Additional "extras" set-ups are in Chapter 7 *Extras for Book*s.

Coffee table books

By far, our favorite books to design are coffee table books. Photography and art books are usually coffee table books. Because they are presenting the work of an artist or photographer, the designer should keep the design more minimalistic to showcase the artwork or photography.

The coffee table book is a book type in which a book designer can add more sparkle and design elements. They are usually large-format books. Like a photography book, it has large images, smaller text size, and uses white space judiciously. This style should have some sort of striking typography or other elements to make it extra special.

While coffee table books should have something special, simple design should be created. If adding additional design elements is in the author's vision, remember that it is their vision that counts. Coffee table books can be quite a bit more work than simpler photography or art books.

The final decision maker is always the author or the person or company paying for the book design. While designers may offer a book layout or design alternative, the surest way to lose the job is to insist that your design is best, whether it is or not. But designers can always make suggestions!

Cookbooks

There is a lot of competition in the marketplace for cookbooks. The author has the pressure of defining their culinary niche with delicious recipes and creative stories or copywriting. The cookbook designer will tie all elements together in a form that needs to stand out from this crowded category.

Consider how this cookbook is different from anything else and play to that distinction.

Not only do individuals write cookbooks, but so do restaurant owners, dieticians, chefs, doctors, celebrities, and people from any walk of life.

Cookbook fractions and type

If the designer has never designed a cookbook before, carefully choose the typeface and fonts for the recipes.

There are special considerations for cookbook design. For instance, use a typeface that has ligatures. You find ligatures in all professional typefaces. To see ligatures in InDesign, go to **Window** > **Type & Tables** > **Glyphs**. Then select 'Fractions'. Alternatively, you can select "Numbers."

Instead of measurements being typeset as in the chart in the left column labeleb "typeset," the measurement should look like those shown in the "professional" column. Some of these characters for the measurements are found in Glyphs. You may have to build off measurements, so make sure the typeface that you select has the characters to needed to create them.

TYPESET	PROFESSIONAL
1/8 cup	⅛ cup
1/2 cup	½ cup
1/3 cup	⅓ cup
2/3 cup	⅔ cup
1/4 cup	¼ cup
3/8 cup	⅜ cup
5/8 cup	⅝ cup
3/4 cup	¾ cup
7/8 cup	⅞ cup

If there are some non-standard measurements that are not in the "Fractions" or "Numbers" glyphs, they can be created. "Standard" glyphs vary from font to font.

Take 5/8 for example. Instead of selecting "Fractions," you can use "Numerators" and "Denominators." Select "Numerators." Select the "5," then select a forward slash "/ " if it exists on the list, or from the keyboard. Now select "Denominators" from the list. Choose "8."

And it is done. It is easy. The result is "⅝."

A COUPLE MORE TIPS

- If fractions need to be built, keep a running list so that each fraction need only be created once. Just copy and paste the fraction as needed.
- Do not add a hyphen between a whole number and a fraction. Example: 2 ⅝ instead of 2-⅝.

Novels

When a novel is set using Adobe InDesign, there is usually something special about the book that makes it more advantageous to use InDesign instead of Microsoft Word.

- Perhaps it is as simple as the author or designer being more comfortable using one software over the other.
- The book may need to be set in a non-standard size.
- There may be process color images that need to be formatted for a higher quality printing than what is supplied by print-on-demand service providers.

There are some excellent and modestly priced Word templates that can be used for the design of a novel.

If using InDesign, the book can be formatted in one document instead of creating a book and adding multiple chapters, unless there are a lot of photographs or graphic images.

Master pages, paragraphs, character styles, and perhaps object styles are created. InDesign is just a more powerful software for book design. But, for a novel that is all text or mostly text, Word can get the job done.

Photography and art books

The guiding principles of a photography or art book is the use of large images, small type, good use of white space, and simple typography. These books are quite often minimalist in their look and feel. The art or photography always takes center stage in the design of this book style. Any other design elements are secondary to the subject of the book—the art or photography.

Such books are always in a large format. A 10 inch by 10 inch square book is a good size, as is 11 or 12 inches square. Books with a portrait or landscape orientation work well too. The largest book size that Star Print Brokers currently prints on press is 12 inches wide by 15 inches in length.

Consider the typical dimensions of the artwork or photography. This does not mean the page and image orientation should match. Depending on the book, you may choose to plan a text block side by side with the image. Conversely, a text block may appear under the image, but it should not appear over an image. Simple design is best.

Picture books

A children's picture book is characterized by use of large images and limited text to tell a story. They may be printed as soft cover or hardcover books. The minimum page count for printing on press is 24 or 32 pages depending on the provider.

We recommend coated paper for a hardcover or soft cover children's book. A dirty fingerprint cannot be wiped off completely, but paper that is coated is better. Uncoated paper will show more grime with usage. However:

POD
Books printed on-demand are output with toner which sits on top of paper. It may smear when wiped with a moist finger.

Printing on press
Books printed on press in signatures use ink which soaks into the paper. It will not smear.

Set the text using Adobe InDesign. Although illustrations are often manipulated in Adobe Illustrator or Adobe Photoshop, resist the temptation to set the type. Only use InDesign to set type.

The best way to layout a children's book is to place the illustrations and then typeset the text to overlay the illustrations. It is easier to control placement of text, margins, type size, and leading for a consistent look on all pages. While this can be done to some degree in Illustrator and Photoshop, every page would need to be adjusted if there are changes. It is easier to make Character and Paragraph Style changes in InDesign.

Illustrated book titles on the cover and spine can cause layout problems on press unless the illustrator follows the cover wrap or dust jacket measurements supplied by the printer. The solution is to typeset the title or make the illustrated title moveable in the document.

Low-res images are a problem. Illustrators that are used to designing for the web versus book printing, often supply the author with images that are too low in effective resolution. If the illustrations were original art instead of created digitally, they must be re-scanned or a new illustration created. Read about resolution in Chapter 1, *Planning a Book*, on pages 60–63.

Page numbering in children's books depends on page count and age group. Picture books of 24 or 32 pages do not need page numbers. Chapter books should have numbered pages.

Soft cover

One concern when writing a low page count soft cover book, may be fitting the title on the spine. There must be enough width on a spine for the book to be perfect bound. That is, the spine will be flat instead of just a stapled fold. The jargon is "stitched" or "saddle stitched."

The page count needed for a spine to be perfect bound depends on the thickness of the paper and the service provider. A book without a spine is often rejected by bookstores. Get the spine thickness from the provider. Take note of the type size and typeface used on the spine to make sure that it is not too small to be easily read.

Hardcover

A book with a hard case is a hardcover book. The material adherred to the outside of the case is called a cover wrap. It is *not* a loose covering, but is glued to the boards. A loose-fitting paper with flaps is a dust jacket.

The material for a cover wrap at POD services is usually either a printed paper cover or a faux cloth cover. However, SPB expanded cover wrap material choices to offer a variety of cloth textures and colors. Suede and faux leather are available at an additional cost. Tell us what you want and request a quote.

When hardcover books have a printed paper cover wrap, the printer will provide measurements to you. They are determined from the book's dimensions, paper thickness, the number of pages, and the printer.

DUST JACKET

Self-publishers choose dust jackets about fifty percent of the time. They are optional, loose fitting, and consist of the images and text for the front cover, back cover, spine, and two flaps. The flaps usually have a book summary, and biography with a photograph of the author on the flaps.

ENDPAPERS

The endpapers are the thick papers glued to the inside front cover and inside back cover of a book. At SPB, they can be printed or not.

If you are not going to print the endpapers, no file is needed because the endpapers will be white, uncoated paper. Let us know if there is a spot ink or CMYK call-out as it is an extra cost to print. We do not need a file for that option, if there is no design on the endpapers.

Board books

Board books are small and limited in page count for babies and toddlers. They usually run 8 to 24 pages and have rounded outside corners. Our company is one of the few that print board books on commercial, offset printing presses.

Babies and children put books in their mouths, so we print with soy-based inks on coated stock. Board books also have a lamination on each page and cover, so the book *can* be wiped off.

Text file

If you are designing a board book, the text file is set-up in one document. It will just be printed on thicker boards rather than paper.

Unlike other types of books where the first page is a right-hand page, a board book's first page is a left-hand page. This page is printed on the inside front cover. You will have an even number of pages in the text document.

The last page of the text file s a right-hand page. The page will be printed on the inside back cover. Go to **File > Document Setup...** and leave the **Facing Pages** box *unchecked*.

DOCUMENT 1: TEXT LAYOUT FOR 16-PAGE BOARD BOOK

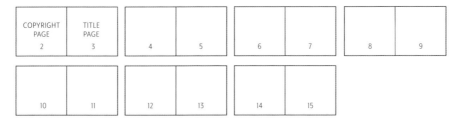

Cover file

Another file is set-up that is the width of the back cover, the spine, plus the front cover. The designer will need to know the spine width of the book which depends on the number of pages and the printer. Not all board books are manufactured on the same equipment or use the same board thickness.

DOCUMENT 2: COVER FILE FOR 16-PAGE BOARD BOOK

Reference books

This is a type of book that is more complex in its design. Charts, especially, take more time to create. Charging a higher design fee for reference books and cookbooks is quite fair given their complexity.

Reference books are usually detailed with charts and graphics that will need to be designed in a way that makes communicating information easier for the reader.

We took over the design and printing of a particular reference book over a dozen years ago. Although we had many years of experience designing books, we learned even more from revising and printing this book once or twice a year. Words of advice for often revised reference books:

- Keep the same look and feel for the cover, provided that it is a successful cover and the author wants to maintain the look for their brand.
- Always use the client's branding. Include their logo, colors, and typefaces.
- Color coding in book sections or chapters helps. Plan the design, but implement it only after the author has approved.
- Use Stylesheets for Paragraphs, Characters and Objects.
- Master pages often prove to be vital for reference books.

It is so important to use the tools within InDesign, so changes can be made globally instead of one instance at a time.

When working with branding, check the Pantone Color Bridge ® against the inks or colors the client uses on their website or on their other printed materials. All too often, the CMYK inks for process color on press do not match the RGB color used on websites and screen monitors.

Since the CMYK ink might not be able to be matched to the client's RGB colors, have this discussion with them. Show them the Pantone Color Bridge for proof. All too often the designer or printer is blamed for a difference in color when it simply cannot be helped. They may lose the job to someone else who cannot replicate the color either.

When taking over a project from someone else, you may find that it is too big a job to do all at once. We made significant changes as we collaborated with our client, but some changes were made in subsequent years. Since the client had a strict deadline, we could not take extra time to overhaul the entire structure of the design in the first year.

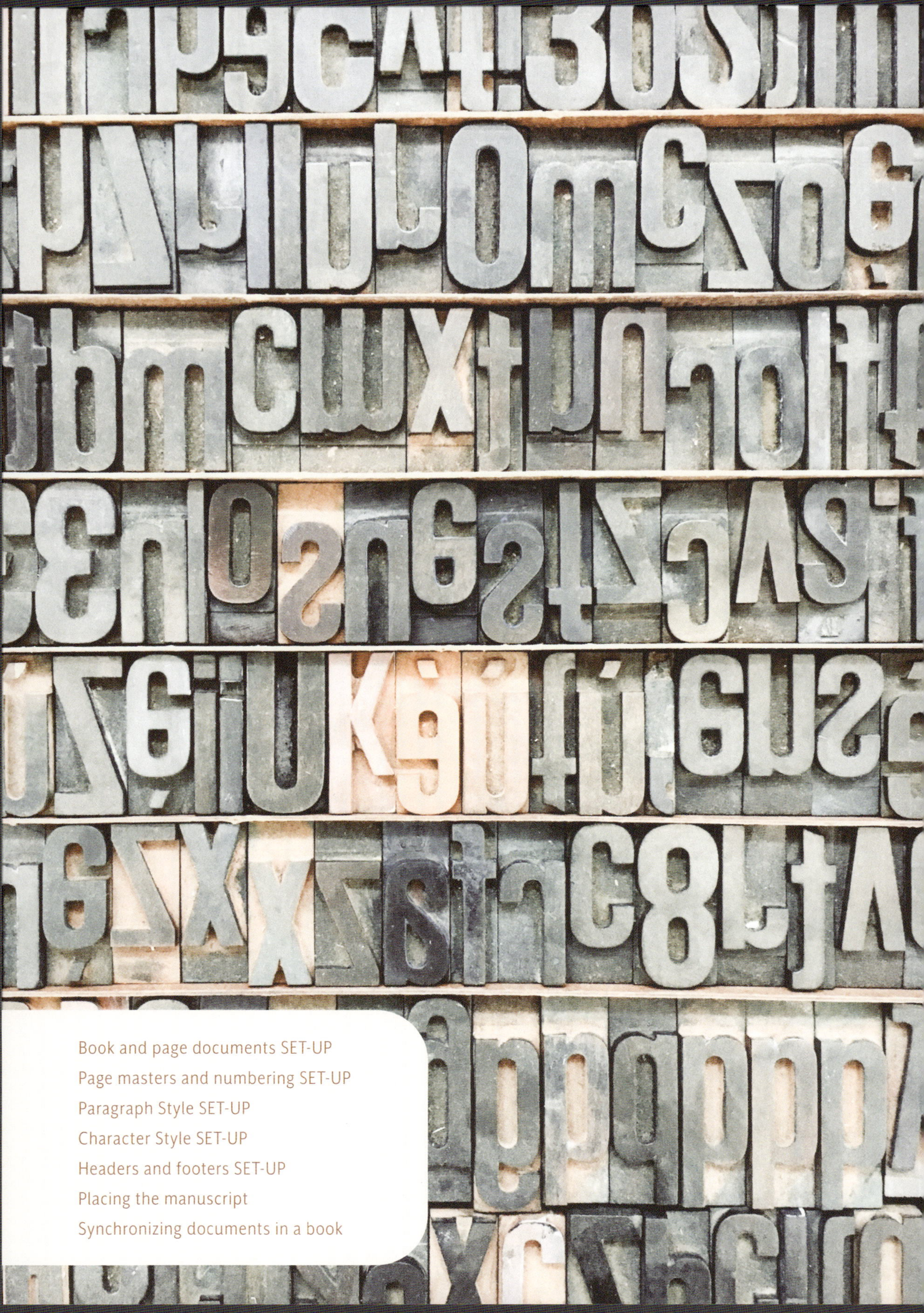

Book and page documents SET-UP

Page masters and numbering SET-UP

Paragraph Style SET-UP

Character Style SET-UP

Headers and footers SET-UP

Placing the manuscript

Synchronizing documents in a book

QUICK START

5

INTERIOR PAGES
Masters and Set-ups

SIMPLICITY IS BEST. Prune words if you are the author. Prune the design if you are the book designer. There is a common tendency to over design. Make it a practice to get away from the design for a few hours or overnight and come back to it with a fresh view. Remove the unnecessary.

Unless stated otherwise, the instructions are for books printing on press with Star Print Brokers.

 QUICK TIPS

- Create a book. Add a Front Matter document, a Chapter 1 document, and if needed, a Back Matter document.
- Read provider documentation before laying out the book.
- If any page bleeds, have *all* pages set to bleed. Add 0.125 inch or 3-millimeter to document set-up bleed setting.
- Design a master page with a basic page layout. Add page numbering and headers or footers as applicable.
- Select typography, creating text and headlines in Paragraph Styles.
- Select CMYK *process color* palette, not *spot color*. Use Pantone Color Bridge Coated, or in Photoshop, select color with eyedropper tool from an image already converted to CMYK.
- Images need to be CMYK, at 300 ppi *or greater, and* at the size they will be when printed *or larger*. It is best to use TIFs or JPGs. However, JPGs can lose resolution. Do not use PNGs as they are for web pages.
- Work in 2-page spreads, adding a spread, or deleting two adjacent pages. Adjust any page discrepancy at the end of a chapter.
- Self-publishers need to buy an ISBN and EAN Bookland barcode once you know the retail price. Bookstores prefer barcodes with the price. A barcode without a price might not be accepted.
- Do not be married to the design. Synchronize masters to change styles globally.

Photo by Favio Santaniello Bruun on Unsplash

BOOK AND PAGE DOCUMENTS

SET-UP

Use this book as an example, or you can use your own book specifications. This is just one way to organize work.

- **Create a folder** for the book, "My Book Title" to store everything that pertains to your book.
- **Create a book**. In InDesign, go to File > New > Book. I named this .indb book file "BOOK DESIGN Simple & Professional BOOK." Add "BOOK" to the end to differentiate the book from the folder. Once the book is created, make sure it is visible in InDesign. If it is not, select Window > and scroll down an see your book title. Select your book.

Create a document

File > New > Document. Select the preset option for print.

- Change Units to Inches.
- Page size, use the size of this book: Width 7 in, Height 10 in.
- Number of Pages: Type 4 and check the Facing Pages box.
- Start of Page #: 1.
- Click the down arrow for Bleed and Slug. If the book has images to bleed, add 0.125 in for Top, Bottom, Inside, and Outside. Optionally, "Inside" may be set to " 0 " in.

Margins can be set in File > Document Setup . . . If any page bleeds, set all documents to bleed.

ALTERNATIVE

You may already have a document open in InDesign. Go to:

- File > Document Setup . . . Select the preset option for print and follow the instructions above.

Graphic artists sometimes say that

they do not see where to add the bleed. "Bleed and Slug" is circled in the first image to the right.

The lower right image shows the "Bleed and Slug" area expanded.

If the book has images that bleed, add 0.125 in for Top, Bottom, Inside, and Outside. Optionally, "Inside" may be set to " 0 " in.

- This will be the first document in your book. It is named here with the initials of the book title: BD 00 Front Matter. Then Save.

ADD A DOCUMENT TO THE BOOK

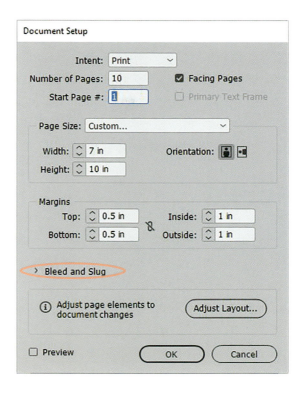

- With the book window open, select the "+" sign to a Add Document. It is circled above, to the left of the "+" sign. Save the book.

If designing a novel with just a few images, creating multiple documents might not be necessary. One InDesign document will do.

Some books have many high-resolution images. Depending on the image sizes, manage larger chapters by breaking content into smaller chapters or documents.

CHANGE FRONT MATTER NUMBER STYLE

- Go to Layout > Numbering & Section Options...

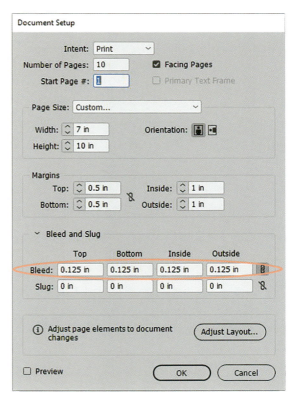

CHAPTER FIVE | INTERIOR PAGES

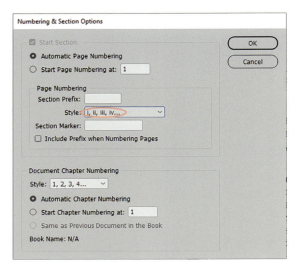

Change front matter number style to Roman.

Create front matter. Highlight to save again as chapter 1.

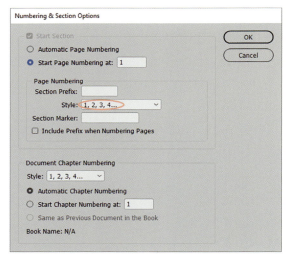

Change chapter 1 number style to Arabic. Start numbering at 1.

Front matter and chapter 1 in this book.

- The front matter numbering uses Roman numerals. Under page numbering, change the [Roman] Style to i, ii, iii, iv . . .

CREATE CHAPTER 1 AND MORE

- Put the cursor on the front matter document to highlight. Go to File > Save as . . . Now rename the new document. I chose the name: BD Ch 01 PLAN Fundamentals.
- In the book window, click the " + " to add that new chapter.
- All chapters and back matter use Arabic numerals. Under page numbering, change the [Arabic] Style to 1, 2, 3, 4 . . .

The number of pages in each document will increase as you add more pages, and it will be different than the example given here.

- Now create chapter 2 by saving Chapter 1 under the new name, "Chapter 2."
- With your cursor on the first page of the chapter, go to Layout > Numbering & Section Options . . . Activate the radio button for "Automatic Page Numbering" if not already active.

Front matter and Chapters 1 and 2 are now saved in the book. Add new chapters by copying Chapter 2 and renaming the new chapter. Because you are using Chapter 2, the page numbering for the rest of the book will be correct.

Note: When you are close to finishing the entire book, know that the total page count is tallied to include the number of pages in the book, plus the number of front matter pages. Make sure you have the correct number of pages to match the printer's quote.

The total number of pages will always be an even number, and the last page in a book will always be a left-hand page.

PAGE MASTERS AND NUMBERING   SET-UP

Start with one Master Page. By default, there are two masters: [None] and Master A. See the Masters Panel which is at the top of the Pages Panel.

Double click the pages icon to the right A-Master highlighted here in blue. The actual Master spread can now be viewed and edited. Notice that the first single page is number 1.

If only all two-page spreads are seen, go to File > Document Set-up ... and check the Facing Pages box.

Add page numbers

Select the Type Tool from the Tools panel. Create a text frame for a number and place it where it should be on all numbered pages.

Go to Type > Insert Special Character > Markers and select Current Page Number.

A default letter A will be seen in the frame because it is the A Master. When the A Master is applied to a page or pages, it will show the actual page number.

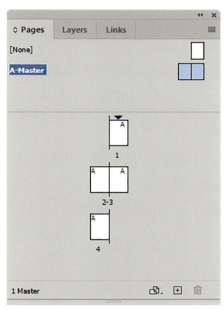

Master A is highlighted and applied to pages 1 through 4.

D   BOOK DESIGN: SIMPLE & PROFESSIONAL

Master D with footer showing page number and book title.

The pages in a chapter may have different masters applied. For instance, the title page in front matter and the first page of a chapter should *not* have visible numbers.

In front matter, drag and drop the [None] Master on page " i ", a right-hand page. This is because front matter is numbered in Roman numerals.

In Chapter 1, drag and drop the [None] Master on page " 1 ", a right-hand page. Chapters and back matter are numbered in Arabic numbers.

Setting Page Margins

Once page margins are determined, double click on [None] and again on Master A and set margins and columns. Also, columns can be set later when setting type. The Masters are the place to add footers or if you prefer, headers alongside the page numbers. The book title is often on all left-hand pages. The right-hand pages often have the chapter or section title.

To apply a Master to a group of pages, click on the three bars at the top right of the Pages Panel to open a drop-down menu. Select Apply Master to Pages . . . and enter the desired page range in "Apply Master."

Paragraph and character styles

Creating and applying paragraph and character styles takes time but will save a great deal of time when changes need to be made globally. It is also helpful to copy and rename a previous book to modify the styles for the new book title. This is not a book on how to use InDesign, but rather on book design. If you need help with these steps, go to Help on the top menu in InDesign.

PARAGRAPH STYLES   SET-UP

Open the Paragraph Styles tab, which is a default on the right side of the application window. Set the [Basic Paragraph] and body text typefaces, sizes, and leading (linespacing).

This is where you will add different sizes of headlines and paragraph styles like "photo title," "photo credit," "recipe," or any style used throughout the document. Give your styles names that make sense to you, so you can quickly apply them.

Try not to over design by creating a new style if an existing style can be used. Creating a style for one-off use is unnecessary and clutters the design.

Staying with a grid is practical for text heavy books, but it does not work well for a book like this, with many changes in text and styles.

A way to adjust text on a grid is to add additional styles with half and quarter size leading. This makes it easy to adjust leading to stay on a grid. For instance, if leading is 16-pt, add an 8-point style and a 4-point style.

These adjustments are not usually needed for novels and text heavy books, or a book that has a great deal of white space, like some photography and art books.

SETTING HALF & QUARTER SIZE LEADING

This book is based on 16-point leading or linespacing for the text:

- For example, add [Basic Paragraph] and Body text Paragraph Styles with 16-point leading.

Half of that is 8-point leading and a quarter is 4-point leading. Fewer changes in linespacing make a better visual impact when following a grid is not possible. Sometimes a little extra leading is needed, but not a full return.

Then:
- Duplicate the style and change leading to 8. Name the Paragraph Style Body text 8-pt leading.
- Duplicate it again and change leading to 4. Name this new Paragraph Style Body text 4-pt leading.

CHARACTER STYLES   SET-UP

Open the Character Styles tab, which is a default on the right side of the application window. What is nice about Character Styles is that you can create a style that only uses one attribute. That way, if you were to change a typeface thoughout the entire book, only that attribute is changed.

SET BOLD, ITALIC, AND ANY OTHER COMMON STYLES

For example, set **bold** and *italic* as different Character Styles. However, try not to use ***bold and italic***. When using **bold**, do not call out the size, leading, or any other style characteristics. Select only the font family and font style.

The font style is "Regular" in this book and the "Bold" font was not bold enough to show differentiation, so the actual font used was "Heavy." By using a Character Style, you can easily change all **bold** type to another font.

Use groups to organize paragraph styles

Many types of books have a limited number of styles. This book is more complicated, so it requires additional organization.

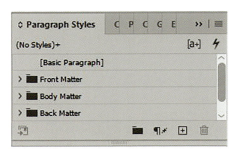

Paragraph Styles group folders

Create New Style Groups to better organize Paragraph Styles. Each group is essentially a folder. Even within a group, you can create other groups and sub-groups.

I often create groups for Front Matter, Body Matter, and if needed, Back Matter. If styles are distinctly different, you can create a new group for each style. But keep things simple.

You will almost always have the same body text, headlines, subheads, page numbers, and footer or header styles throughout the book.

Whatever you do in one section or chapter, you will want to have available in all documents in the book. The easiest way to accomplish this is to *synchronize* documents. See instructions on page 100 in this chapter.

HEADERS AND FOOTERS   SET-UP

The more detailed the book, the more work it is to create running headers and footers. Start by looking through other books that are similar in size, content, and perhaps subject matter to the book you are designing. Decide what is functional for the reader. Determine what is necessary for the book's design. The material in the book should dominate, not the headers or footers. They are only a functional or ornamental guide for the reader.

Running headers and footers are displayed at the top and bottom of pages. I have also seen them running vertically, Typically, the running head or is at the top of the page and the running footer is at the bottom. Use one or the other, but not both. They can contain the title of the book, a part or section of a book, a chapter, or any other reference point. They also contain the page number.

Headers or footers if used, are on most, but not all pages. If you previously created a master with a page number, this is where to add your header or footer. Refer to the illustration on page 95 for a sample page number and footer set-up.

Character Styles or Paragraph Styles should be created for headers or footers and page numbers. Since the book title is on the left page and chapter on the right page of a spread, you will need to save the first master as "A Master Ch 1." Duplicate this master renaming it to "B Master Ch 2" and change the chapter name on the right-hand page. The A, B, C, etc. are automatically generated in In Design. You need only add an identifying word to the name of the master.

Special placement

There are pages where it is accepted practice not to place running headers and footers. The title page and copyright page for instance, need not have them at all. It looks cluttered. The first page of a chapter does not have a page number. Reference the front matter and back matter in this book, as correct use and placement is indicated in grey type at the bottom of each page.

Many book designers tend to over design. Take a fresh look at your design and remove what is not necessary. This applies to anything you create when designing a book, including the design of headers, footers, and also page numbers.

Functionality of headers and footers

Children's picture books and board books need not have any headers and footers or even page numbers. The exception would be if the book has a large page count. Then, you just use a page number.

Novels and most other books, by default, have a stationery folio (page number) and header or footer consisting of the book title on the left-hand page. The right-hand page has the chapter title and, optionally, the chapter number or section within the chapter. It is a matter of how you wish to design the book.

Books with weighty subject matter should consider using the left-hand page footer or header for the chapter, and the right-hand page footer or header for each individual section.

Highly detailed manuals or reference books may opt to use the left-hand page for the sections, and the right-hand page for specific material on the page or pages.

Placing the manuscript

There are several ways to handle formatting of the manuscript in the Microsoft Word document and the Adobe InDesign document. Frankly, they can be quite complicated, and since we want a simple yet professional book, I suggest the easiest method below.

Easy—Microsoft Word into Adobe InDesign

Process: The least complicated way to do this is copying and pasting the text from the Microsoft Word manuscript into InDesign.

Simply go to File > Place. It can be copied and placed all at once in just one document or break it up into different Chapter files in the book which is created in InDesign. Go to File > New and select Book.

Result: When you place the file this way, the Microsoft formatting is lost. You will need to go through the manuscript and apply formatting to words and paragraphs, italics, footnotes, headers, and subheading typefaces, etc.

Be sure to first create Adobe InDesign Paragraph and Character Styles. Then format the text after it is placed in InDesign. It is helpful to work with InDesign and the Word documents side-by-side on your monitor.

Synchronizing documents in a book

Changes are inevitable, so we frequently synchronize documents. Adobe InDesign made it easy to do synchronization globally. It would be great if each master, paragraph stylesheet, and all fonts chosen in the beginning of the design process were the final choices. However, book design is a process, and sometimes we simply change our minds.

The synchronization of all documents in the book is a huge time saver. Avoid going into each chapter to make changes.

Assuming the InDesign book is now created and has several documents that may be front matter, chapter 1, chapter 2, back matter, or similarly named documents. Frequently save chapters. Save the book with a right click on the three horizontal lines and select "Save".

HOW TO SYNCHONIZE DOCUMENTS

- With the book open and documents placed in the book, click on the three horizonal lines in the upper right corner and select Synchronize Options...

- Make sure that Other and Styles and Swatches are checked, and all of the items in each of these two groups are also checked. This need only be verified once.
- Please refer again to the illustration above. See the style source icon that is circled and next to "BD 00 Front Matter." Let's say that we changed or added a Paragraph Style, Character Style or even a Master page in this first document. We want to synchronize the rest of the documents in the book so the styles match.
- Press Ctrl (Windows) or Command (Mac) and click the rest of the documents. Leave the "BD 00 Front Matter" document alone because it is the source document in this case.
- Again, click on the three horizonal lines in the upper right corner and select Synchronize Book.
- All Other and Styles and Swatches styles from "BD 00 Front Matter" are synced to the rest of the chapters. The style source icon can be placed next to other chapters that you want to synchronize.
- For instance, if you are working in "BD 07 Extras" and realize that you want to change the color of a Paragraph Style, simply change the color of the style in that document only.
- Click the empty box to the left of "BD 07 Extras" and the style source icon will appear there. It becomes the source document. Now, click all the other documents and synchronize.

Note: You might want to change, for example, all the footer placements in all of the chapter Masters. Select any chapter, like Chapter 3 for example, and place the style source icon there. Simply change all the Masters in Chapter 3 and then synchronize all other documents in the book to Chapter 3.

Book cover design
Spine width and printers templates
Soft cover InDesign file SET-UP
Hardcover with printed cover wrap SET-UP
Hardcover with cover wrap material SET-UP
Wire-O bindings SET-UP
Standard dust jacket SET-UP

COVER DESIGN & BINDING

QUICK START

THE TYPEFACES AND OVERALL STYLE OF A COVER do not have to match a book's interior pages. Quite often the cover and interior text of a book are designed by different designers.

    Self-publishers can create a beautiful cover with only image(s) and type. But, if you have a highly creative idea in mind, hire an illustrator or a high-end designer who specifically designs covers. Their fee could be several hundred dollars, a thousand dollars, or more. Beware of $50 covers!

    Designing a cover includes different design features, depending on the binding style of the book. In this chapter, we will cover the binding styles and how the InDesign set-up is created for each.

 QUICK TIPS

- Choose the book printer and finalize the written quote including page count, so that specifications are clear.
- Know the dimensions of the book and the binding style. It is helpful to know the final page count and paper thickness for the spine design too. But the spine width can be adjusted later if necessary.
- The front cover of a soft cover book is almost always the same dimensions as the book's interior page size.
- The front cover of a hardcover book is always larger than the book's interior page size, because of the boards used for the hard case. The specific size is not identical across printers.

BOOK COVER DESIGN   SET-UP

The design of the cover of a book is an art. However, the purpose of *Book Design: Simple & Professional* is to provide information to make book design as simple as possible for a novice, and still have a professional looking book. Most important of all, the book must have a cover that sells.

Photo by Kelly Sikkema on Unsplash, digitally altered in Photoshop by Nancy Starkman

Whether selling a book online or for print, envision the cover as a thumbnail image. Is the book title large enough to read if listed for sale on Amazon, on a website, or in a book review or testimonial? Does the typography, treatment of the title, and photograph or graphic image convey the right message to potential book buyers?

ISBN and barcode

ISBN

The International Standard Book Number (ISBN) is a unique commercial book identifier.

Do not confuse it with an ASIN which stands for Amazon Standard Identification Numbers that contains 10 letters and/or numbers that identify an Amazon product. For Amazon's purposes, a book's ASIN is the same as the ISBN. Yet, if you are selling books in a bookstore, an author or self-publisher needs their own ISBN, not an ASIN.

Each ISBN identifies a book. Therefore, if the formats are an ebook and a soft cover, you will need two ISBNs. The ISBN has 13 digits. Any ISBN bought before January 1, 2007 has 10 digits.

A Bookland EAN barcode is mandatory in most bookstores. It is generated specifically for ISBNs. You can buy an ISBN or a pack of ten at ISBN.org. While you can buy a plain UPC, or Universal Product Code, your book would not appear in bookstore and related databases. A UPC is for general merchandise, not books.

Here is what you get when you buy an ISBN:

- Identification of one book in one format
- Get Into Books In Print
- Register yourself as The Publisher
- Appearance in relevant databases

A WORD OF CAUTION ABOUT PRINT ON-DEMAND

Buy the ISBN and barcode yourself, as you should be the publisher of your book. That way, you retain all profits. If an on-demand publisher provides this ISBN, they are the publisher. You will receive only royalties, which pay less than the profit you could be making. Also, they are the publisher of record, and that means you are not. Read contracts before signing!

CAUTIONARY TALE ABOUT AN UNSCRUPULOUS ISBN SELLER

This was a situation in which an author bought an ISBN from a person for $40. This was a huge red flag, and we had a talk with our client.

The author went back to the seller asking the all-important question: "Who is the publisher of my book?" The seller said, "It would be okay." But it was not okay. The seller would be the publisher of the author's book had our client used the seller's ISBN. Instead he bought his own ISBN. You should pay $125 for one ISBN at the time of publishing of this book.

Barcode

If you buy a barcode with an ISBN purchased previously, you must register your title information at ISBN.org.

BARCODE SIZE

The barcode size is standard at 92 percent of the full-size image but can be as small as 80 percent of the original size. This assumes that the barcode is purchased though ISBN.org.

PLACEMENT

The placement of the barcode is predetermined. It is standard to be in the lower right corner on the back cover. This makes it easier for bookstores to scan the barcode.

Adjust the placement to not fall into the hinge or too close to the spine. It is a good idea to put barcodes on the book ifself as well as the dust jacket. This is just in case a dust jacket is lost or damaged.

Retail price

Be sure to use the suggested retail price in the barcode. Most bookstores will not accept a book without the retail price in the barcode.

Amazon wants to sell books at a significant discount off that retail price. We recommend setting a higher retail price on your book to offset the deep Amazon discount and their fees. If selling online on your own website, add a shipping and handling fee in addition to the price of the book. You do not want to cut too deeply into an already discounted price.

Check out the competition. When you do, check the copyright date and any printing date on the copyright page of a similar book. You want a similar binding, page count, and printing date to compare to your book.

Just remember, you can always put a book on sale. But to increase the retail price of your book means buying a new barcode, printing the new price on stickers, and then applying the stickers to the books.

Spine width and printers' templates

The page count is important. The printer needs the final page count, binding type, and paper type and weight to determine the spine width. Then a measurement guide can be provided to the book designer so they can lay out the book cover, including proper sizing of the title on the spine.

The printer may provide a diagram showing the measurements for the specific type of cover. If the book is a simple soft cover, only the spine width is provided, with no diagram. That is because the front and back cover of a soft cover book are the same dimensions as the interior pages.

Files are set up in InDesign and in a separate file from the book's interior pages. Templates simply show the measurements on a diagram. It is usually not provided in an InDesign document.

Make sure that you relay any relevant changes to the printer before you request a template. The measurements can also vary depending on the printer or service provider used.

Soft cover

A soft cover book is also called a paperback book. However, soft cover books do not have to be manufactured like a cheap dime store novel. They can be a higher quality book printed in process color on a thicker coated stock.

The text pages can be the same as the interior pages in a hardcover book with the only difference being the binding. In fact, we get orders for a minimum 1,000 hardcover copies plus and printing simultaneously, 1,000 or more additional soft cover copies.

Our minimum at Star Print Brokers is 1,000 hardcover or 2,000 soft cover books. Sometimes authors split or combine orders. For instance, you could print 1,000 hardcover and 500 soft cover copies, provided the books are printed at the same time and shipped together. Our books are custom manufactured. If you need a variation on quantity, discuss the possibility with a representative.

SOFT COVER INDESIGN FILE

SET-UP

A soft cover is also known as a paperback book. Open a new document. For now, **we will assume the book is 7 inches wide x 10 inches tall. The spine width is 0.5 inch, and the cover image will bleed.** To bleed means that the image extends beyond the trim of the cover, and 0.125 inch will be trimmed off all four sides of the printed cover file.

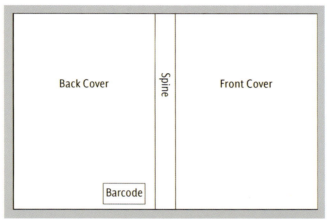

Soft cover book cover. No bleeds are visible in this image.

- Go to File > New > Document.
- Number of Pages: 1
  Here is how we got to the total width:
  7 in back cover + 0.5 in spine + 7 in front cover = 14.5 in
- Width: 14.5 in   Height: 10 in
- Click the bleed and slug down arrow. Set Top, Bottom, Inside, and Outside Bleed to 0.125 in or 3 mm. If there is no bleed, set Top, Bottom, Inside, and Outside Bleed to 0 in or 0 mm.

See soft cover French flap AdobeInDesign set-up in Chapter 7, *Extras for Book*s on pages 124 to 125.

HARDCOVER WITH PRINTED COVER WRAP

SET-UP

This cover wrap is printed on press versus a material cover wrap. There is an outside margin of about 15 to 20 millimeters or about 0.75 inches, depending on the manufacturer. The 0.75 inch margin is on all four sides. The cover wrap is glued to the boards.

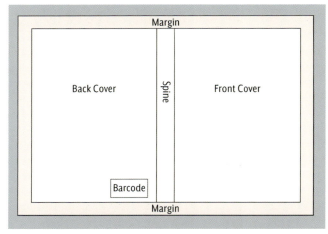

Hardcover for cover wrap to print on press. Images and text do not fall into margin.

THE EXTENSION OF BACKGROUND ART:

The background needs to extend all the way into the outside margins. The cover wrap is folded over the boards and glued down.

Only the background can be extended into the margin area. If anything else extends, like the title or dominant image, it will *not* be seen. That is because the margin wraps is glued to the inside front and back covers. The endpapers are then glued over the margins of the cover wrap.

Open a new document. For now, **we will assume the book is 7 inches wide x 10 inches tall. The spine width is 0.5 inch, and the cover wrap margin is .75 inches on all four sides.**

- Go to File > New > Document.
- Number of Pages: 1
  Here is how we got to the measurements:
  Width: 0.75 in margin + 7 in back cover + 0.5 in spine + 7 in front cover + 0.75 in margin = 16 in
  Height: 0.75 in margin + 10 in tall covers + 0.75 in margin = 11.5 in
- Width: 16 in   Height: 11.5 in

HARDCOVER WITH COVER WRAP MATERIAL SET-UP

Hardcover book cover dimensions may differ among printers. A measurement template to use for book cover wrap dimensions is needed for any hardcover book. Ask for measurements or a template from the printer. The cover wrap file is a separate InDesign file from the actual text pages.

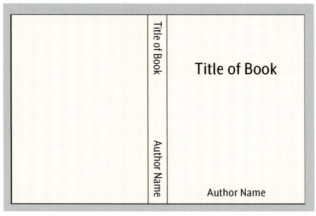

Book cover in black and white for a foil stamp die, to stamp a foil on hardcover material.

VERY IMPORTANT

The printing file will be black and white with no background color or images. That is because you are creating the InDesign file for a die to create a foil stamp. You are not printing ink on the cover of a book with a material cover wrap. Select the foil with the printing representative.

COVER WRAP IS NOT THE SAME THING AS A DUST JACKET

The choice is between a cloth cover wrap or a printed paper cover wrap. Any cover wrap is glued to the boards. A dust jacket is never glued. It is a loose paper that folds around the book. The dust jacket flaps are tucked around the front and inside back covers. We manufacture standard and French fold styles.

    Hardcover books can be bound with a printed paper cover wrap, cloth, or other materials. There is extra margin that extends beyond the cover, but only for printed covers, not material covers. This margin wraps over the top, bottom, and outside edges of the book. When designing for a material cover wrap, you do not need to set up the InDesign file with any extra wrapping margins.

CHAPTER SIX | COVER DESIGN & BINDING   109

WORKING WITH HARDCOVER DIMENSIONS FOR THE COVER

When a hardcover book is 7" x 10", we are stating the dimensions of the page. The boards extend out farther than the pages. But if asking for a quote, we still say the book is 7" x 10".

In the USA, book designers typically work in units of inches or picas. However, in Europe and Asia, they work in millimeters. In Preferences, toggle between millimeters, inches, or picas as needed.

Either right click on the rulers to change to millimeters, for instance, or go to Edit > Preferences > Units & Increments. Change the horizontal and vertical to millimeters. Click OK.

Open a new document. For now, **we will assume the book is 7 inches wide x 10 inches tall. The spine width is 0.5 inch.**

Note: The dimensions below are the example text page dimensions. However, all hardcover dimensions will be larger than the page size. This is because the boards are larger. Board dimensions and thickness varies among printers.

- Go to File > New > Document.
- Number of Pages: 1
  Here is how we got to the measurements:
  Width: 7 in back cover + 0.5 in spine + 7 in front cover = 14.5 in.
- Width: 14.5 in   Height: 10 in

Under File > Document Setup, set the width to 14.5", and the height to 10". Ignore the Bleed and Slug settings for material cover wrap files.

THE BARCOCDE AND COVER WRAP

A material cover wrap usually does not have a barcode on the back cover. That is because it most often has a dust jacket printed with the barcode. If you do not want the hardcover book with a material cover wrap to have a dust jacket. A barcode sticker must be printed separately to be applied to the back cover of the book. It can also be applied to a shrink-wrapped book or a poly bag especially for that book.

However, do not bag or shrink-wrap books if they are to be sold in bookstores. Book buyers like to browse books before buying and this feature may discourage sales.

WIRE-O BINDINGS

SET-UP

Wire-O bindings are better than spirals and are about the same cost. Wires come in quite a few colors and diameters.

See images of Wire-O bindings in Chapter 8, *Printing on Press*, pages 148 to 149. Also, read the preceding pages about hardcover material cover wrap, hardcover, printed cover wrap, and soft cover books, as the same information often applies.

Open Wire-O

The standard Wire-O binding has no spine, which is needed if books are to be sold in bookstores. A standard Wire-O can have a hardcover or soft cover.

SOFT COVER SET-UP

Easy! Simply design the front cover and back covers just as you would any interior book page. The covers are the same size as the text pages. However, they need to be provided in a separate file, unless the book is "self-cover". This is because the cover paper weight will be a different stock and heavier weight than the text stock.

HARDCOVER SET-UP

Ask the service provider for a template or measurements for these bindings. Although there is no spine, the covers are larger than the pages. Three things to watch out for are:

- If the covers print, you will need to add the extra margin on top, bottom, and sides for the board wrapping area.
- Be careful not to put content in the margins that fold over the boards. Only background color or undefined images can extend into the background.
- Because it is a hardcover book, even if it has no spine, the inside front and back covers have endpapers. By default, the endpapers are white paper. However, they may be printed or a specialty stock for an additional cost.

Semi-concealed Wire-O

The semi-concealed Wire-O can have the wire running through the spine or on the back cover next to the spine. This applies to hardcover and soft cover book bindings. **Ask the service provider for a template or measurements for these bindings and any hardcover endpaper measurements.**

Concealed Wire-O

The concealed Wire-O is hidden in the space behind the spine.

The endpapers for Wire-O hardcovers are not like regular hardcover endpapers because of the construction of this binding style. **Ask the service provider for a template or measurements for these bindings and any hardcover endpaper measurements.**

STANDARD DUST JACKET   SET-UP

A dust jacket is a loose paper wrapping for a hard case or perfect bound book. Also called a dust jacket, it has an inside front cover and an inside back cover flap. The jacket and flaps usually contain promotional information. You may want to add a summary of the book on one flap. An author biography is often placed on the other flap.

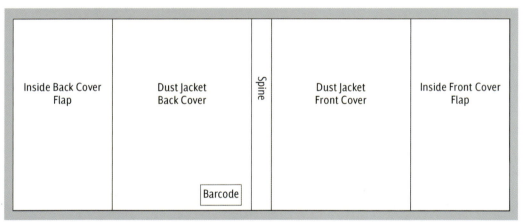

Standard dust jacket set-up

The jacket is printed on a commercial printing press just as the text of a book is printed. Then, a lamination is applied to the jacket. The lamination can be gloss or matte, depending on the style of the book or the author's preference. The cost is the same for either matte or gloss lamination.

You may add embellishments to a dust jacket for added value.

Delivering a higher quality book to readers means that self-publishers can charge a higher retail price. Perhaps a dust jacket may cost the self-publisher and extra 50 cents to a dollar or more per copy. It is important not only to consider the cost of optional items, but also how much more a self-publisher can charge for a hardcover book.

If a dust jacket or any other item costs 50 cents per book you might add one dollar added to the retail price. You can actually make 50 cents more per book in this scenario. The self-publisher or author should decide if it is worth it. Will you still stay competitively priced in the marketplace? Usually, yes, as the extra item adds value.

We can also add a spot varnish, spot UV, or even a silk UV printed over the lamination on the jacket. For instance, you can have just one image, an area of type (the title) stand out with a spot varnish. Spot varnish is applied to a defined area. Flood varnish covers the entire area. Jackets can also be embossed, having raised type or other design areas. You can even add foil stamping in a variety of colors. We usually have both matte and gloss finishes for foils. We provide a custom dust jacket template for your book

Sometimes self-publishers search for a template for book jackets. Book dimensions, spine width, page count, and paper thickness vary. That is why we cannot post a dust jacket template. But you can prepare a preliminary file yourself in InDesign, as long as you are prepared to modify it before printing. Star Print Brokers will supply a specific template in millimeters, for the dust jacket style you choose.

See the French fold dust jacket set-up in Chapter 7, *Extras for Books*, on pages 125 to 126.

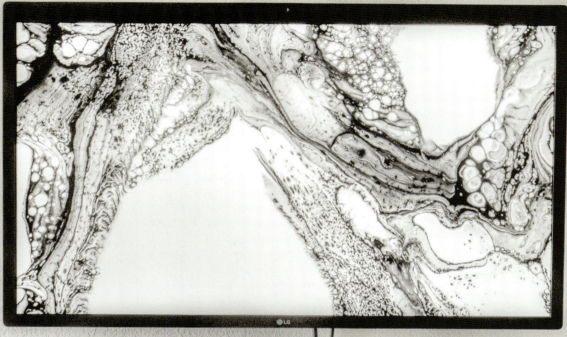

- Printed endpapers SET-UP
- Duotones SET-UP
- Slip cases
- Bumper boxes
- Head and tail bands
- Ribbon markers
- Lamination
- Soft cover French flaps SET-UP
- French fold dust jacket SET-UP
- Vellum tip-in sheet
- Belly Band
- Tip-on cover sticker SET-UP
- Spot varnish SET-UP
- Foil emboss / stamp SET-UP
- Book sleeve
- Journal with elastic band
- Hardcover endpaper pockets

EXTRAS FOR BOOKS
Unique Finishes

THERE ARE MANY OPTIONS AVAILABLE for book printing and binding. However, options are limited with print-on-demand, or if printing on press with a company unlike Star Print Brokers. Most services use block lettering on the spine of a hardcover book instead of the designer created spine lettering. Also, they might not offer spot varnish, French flaps, or many of the other options available at SPB.

QUICK TIPS

- Check with the service to see if they have the options you want.
- Extras add to the cost. Ask that they be listed as separate line items. Quotes should be customized. Request a ballpark quote for the book and quantity first along with maybe one or two options. After reviewing the rough quote, then you may request additional options.
- Do not design a book until you select the printer.

Printed endpapers

An endpaper, also called an endsheet, glues to the inside front and back covers of a hard case book.

If they do not print, endpapers will remain the color of the paper. Uncoated stock is standard for endpapers, but they can also print on coated stock or specialty paper.

Endpapers in a book printed on a commercial printing press

Endpapers: POD books

POD hardcover books often are not bound in the same way as traditional book printing and binding. The endsheet of a print-on-demand book may be one page wide.

Photo by Andre Jasso on Unsplash

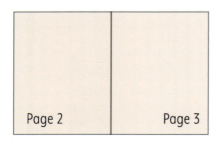
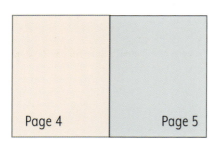
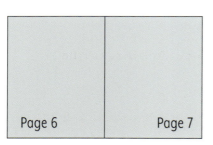

Endpapers: Books printing on press

Professionally bound books printing on press have endpapers that are twice the width of a text page. One or both sides of the endsheet may print, or they may be blank. If blank, no InDesign file or PDF is required.

Endpapers are a fine and relatively inexpensive enhancement. They add an elegant finishing touch to hardcover books. The right color or design can help to make the book unique and especially attractive.

A specialty paper stock, foil stamp, or blind embossing can also add interest and style.

THE ENDPAPER LAYOUT

Page 1. Glued to inside of front cover (blank)
Page 2. Inside front cover (left page on spread)
Page 3. Facing page (right page on spread)
Page 4. Page facing the text block

The text block is between the front and back endpapers (pink and gray in diagram).

Page 5. Page facing the text block
Page 6. Facing back cover (left page on spread)
Page 7. Inside back cover (right page on spread)
Page 8. Glued to inside of back cover (blank)

Presenting the final PDF in this manner eliminates any source of confusion for the printer regarding pagination of endpapers.

The InDesign set-up often causes confusion. Just remember, the endpaper art should be in a separate file from the interior text.

While simple one-color endsheets are easy to designate with just a 4C callout or a PMS code, this is a foolproof way to present the endsheets file no matter how complicated the content might be.

Create an 8-page file as pictured on the previous page. When making the PDF, add all printer's marks including trim marks. Also add a 3 mm or 0.125 inch bleed if necessary, and color bars.

Lay out the eight pages with page 1 as a right-hand page. The diagram on the opposite page shows the ends before the text in pink. The endpapers after the text are gray in the diagram.

Pages 4 and 5 split so that pages 1, 2, 3, and 4 are in the front of the book. Pages 5, 6, 7, and 8 are in the back of the book.

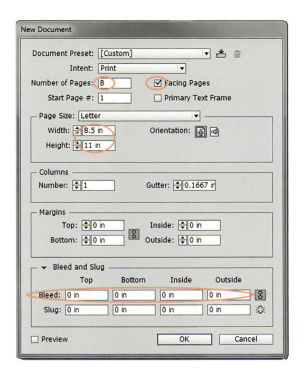

PRINTED ENDPAPERS INDESIGN FILE   SET-UP

Open a new document. Endpapers should not be in the text file.
- Go to File > New > Document.
- Number of Pages: 8. Check Facing Pages box.
- The Width and Height should be the same page dimensions as the book's text page size.
- Click the bleed and slug down arrow. If the endpapers bleed, set Top, Bottom, Inside, and Outside Bleed to 0.125 in or 3 mm. If there is no bleed, set Top, Bottom, Inside, and Outside Bleed to 0 in or 0 mm.

The printer needs PDFs to print from, not InDesign files. Make the PDF for endpapers or text pages using Adobe Acrobat® with the "Export as" radio button for "Pages" checked. See Chapter 8 *Printing on Press*, page 152.

Duotones

Self-publishers and designers can create duotones for print production on printing presses. Print a black and white photography book with a different visual impact.

You see in the images below, that the photo on the left is in color. The photo on the right is the same image, but converted to a duotone. The duotone is an image printed in black plus one other Pantone Matching System (PMS) ink.

Process color photograph

Duotone photograph with two spot ink

Image format in 8-bit PSD, TIF or JPG, not 16-bit

Images or photographs can be in a .psd, .tif or .jpg format. In Adobe InDesign, you can link to the image file that has been converted to a duotone.

We say that a logo or another image is in full 4-color process, also known as CMYK. If already using a duotone of black plus one PMS, the color image will automatically make book printing a 5-color job. That changes the quote and increases the cost. Instead of 2-color printing for duotones, (black (K) plus the selected Pantone ink) it will become 4-color process CMYK plus the 1 Pantone ink.

Start with 8-bit images. It is the standard and what we recommend, not 16-bit images.

DUOTONES

SET-UP

1. Convert to Grayscale by going to Image > Mode > Grayscale.
2. Once converted to Grayscale, you have the option in the same menu to select Image > Mode > Duotone.
3. A new Duotone Options dialog box will open. Under Type, select Duotone. Then select the two inks you want to use.

Most often, the first ink is black. Make sure it is the black from the correct color library, Pantone Solid Coated for coated paper, or Pantone Solid Uncoated for uncoated paper. *Be careful which color library you select.*

These libraries do not designate paper stock to be gloss or matte. Before you select the library, either check the final book printing quote or contact your printer to verify paper selection.

Very Important:
Choose process black, which is 100 percent black (K=100).

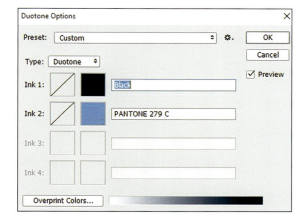

To select the second duotone ink, click on the box on the right. For the photo in our sample image, we selected Pantone 279 C.

If you want to save this Preset, simply click on the little wheel to the right of the preset that now says "Custom". Give it a new name if you wish, and your duotone set-up will always be there for you. This is especially useful if you are doing the entire book in one duotone Pantone Matching System (PMS) color plus Process Black.

If the final image seems a little dark as compared to the grayscale original, two suggestions follow.

You can 1) select a lighter secondary ink or 2) create a curve setting. You will be able to adjust each image with an individualized curve setting. Read more about curve settings at Adobe Photoshop help.

When working with a duotone, or any image, be sure to understand resolution and effective resolution.

Slip cases

A book slip case is simply a box open on just the spine side. It can be made for a single book or for sets of two or more volumes. **We only sell slip cases with book orders.** Slip cases can be manufactured so that both narrow ends are open, but that is unusual.

Book in slip case

A fine photography or art book is that much more beautiful when it comes in a book slip case. If you have a high page count book, break the book up into two or more volumes and present them in a slip case.

A variety of materials

Hardcover coffee table books might have a cover wrap that is printed, faux cloth or faux leather, real cloth or bonded leather. The book may have a standard dust jacket. If you want to really set it apart, add a French fold dust jacket. The slip case can be in the same material or something different. Soft cover or paperback books with a flat spine can also be in a slip case. Design it anyway you wish, but before finalizing the design, it is wise to get a quote.

Most often the slip case has a blind stamp or a foil stamp. Some also have a permanent adhesive, printed sticker, called a tip-on image. A matte lamination or UV coating is usually added.

A book slip case is an inexpensive luxury

Suppose that 1,000 hardcover books are ordered. Just 100 to 500 slip cases can be ordered at the same time. The author may want a regular edition book and a premium edition. The premium edition sells for a higher price.

A slip case cannot be ordered as a one-off standalone item. They are manufactured with the book for the best fit. Adding a few dollars for a slip case can increase the retail price of the book by quite a bit more than the cost without a slip case.

Ask provider for slip case measurement template.

Bumper boxes

This is a box that is custom manufactured at the same time as the book is being printed. **We only sell bumper boxes with book orders.** The bumpers as seen in this photo, are on either side of the book that is placed in the box.

A bumper box can have a plain white exterior as seen in the photo, or it can be kraft paper as seen on the interior of the box.

Bumper box with book inside

The outside of the bumper box can be printed too. A beautiful treatment is to have the outside printed with the same design as might be used on the endpapers of the book.

You may request that the book be placed into the bumper box with box left unsealed.

With an unsealed bumper box, a bill of sale, a thank you, a letter, or extra marketing slips can be placed inside. The author would then seal the bumper box with a wide strip of sealing tape so the box is almost ready to mail or ship.

A book is placed inside another bumper box style

The finishing touch is addressing the box. Some options are:

- FedEx or UPS label affixed to the front of the bumper box.
- Affix your own mailing label.
- Print a mailing label to go with the outside design of the box.
- Write the address in an area left blank.

Note: If addresses will be handwritten, discuss this with the printer to see if a coated or uncoated stock would be best to use, and will not smear.

Ask provider for bumper box measurement template.

Head and tail bands

The little pieces of colored fabric found on the top and bottom of a hardcover book spine are head and tail bands. They cannot be used on soft cover books. The bands come in quite a few solid colors and two colors on one band.

Gray and white head and tail bands. This example is a cloth covered book with a dust jacket. It is a hardcover book with a square-back binding,

Head and tail bands are strictly for ornamentation but found on most hardcover books with professional quality binding. Star Print Brokers includes them in all hardcover quotes. Removing the bands from the quote will not change the cost at all.

If a sewn-in ribbon marker is desired, the color should coordinate with the head and tail bands.

Notice that the book on the left has a square spine. The book on the opposite page has a round spine.

The bands and ribbon markers are not typical with most print-on-demand services.

Head and tail band examples

122 BOOK DESIGN: SIMPLE & PROFESSIONAL

Ribbon markers

Bookmarks are called ribbon markers and are sewn into hardcover books. Head and tail bands should match or coordinate with the ribbon marker. In the photo, the author chose an orange ribbon marker to go with white head and tail bands. The color combination matches their logo and the design of the book.

A ribbon marker is great for notebooks and journals with elastic bands. They are wonderful to keep your place in a cookbook. Larger cookbooks often have two ribbon markers sewn in. It makes any book that much more special.

A ribbon marker is useful to hold the reader's place as well as decorative.

Ribbon markers come in different widths and colors. A rough texture is available, as are satin and *gros grain* ribbons. Some styles such as the satin ribbons, can be imprinted with text, a quote or company name or a logo.

Just like head and tail bands, the ribbon marker is not typically found with on-demand services.

An orange ribbon marker with white head and tail bands. This book has a printed cover wrap and no dust jacket. It is a hardcover with a round-back binding.

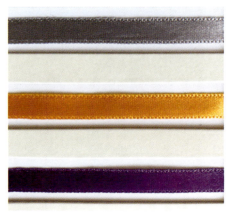

Ribbon marker examples

Lamination

A choice of either matte or gloss lamination is included in the cost for a printed cover wrap, standard dust jacket, French fold dust jacket, or the cover of a soft cover book.

Matte Soft Touch lamination is also offered for an additional cost.

CHAPTER SEVEN | EXTRAS FOR BOOKS   123

Soft cover French flaps

French flaps are formed by the extension of the front and/or back covers of a soft cover book. There can be one or two French flaps and they are functional as well as decorative. The cover is printed on heavier stock.

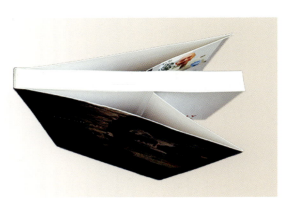

A soft cover book with French flaps on both the front and cover covers. You may opt to have just one flap on either the front or back cover.

A biography of the author and a summary can be added to the flaps, just as on the dust jacket of a hard-cover book.

Some self-publishers prefer to leave flaps blank. Another treatment is to add a logo. If an embossed type or foil stamp is being added to the cover, then foiling, or embossing the logo on the flaps is usually no extra cost.

The width of a flap can be nearly as wide as the book. This also depends on the book dimensions, therefore, the sheet size on press. Adding flaps is a custom option not found at most print-on-demand services.

SET-UP

Open a new document. For now, let us assume the book is 7" wide x 10" tall, and there are 5" flaps on the front and back covers. The spine width is 0.5 inch, and the cover image will bleed. To bleed means that 0.125" will be trimmed off on all sides of the printed image.

- Go to File > New > Document.
- Number of Pages: 1
  Here is how we got to the width:
  5 in back flap + 7 in back cover + 0.5 in spine + 7 in front cover + 5 in + front flap = 24.5 in
- Width: 24.5 in   Height: 10 in.
- Click the bleed and slug down arrow. Set Top, Bottom, Inside, and Outside Bleed to 0.125 in or 3 mm. If there is no bleed, set Top, Bottom, Inside, and Outside Bleed to 0 in or 0 mm.
  See soft cover set-up, Chapter 6, *Book Cover Design & Binding,* page 107.

| Back Cover Flap | Back Cover | Spine | Front Cover | Front Cover Flap |

(Barcode shown on Back Cover)

The set-up for a soft cover book with French flaps

French fold dust jacket

A French fold dust jacket has an extra flap on the top and bottom of the dust jacket. After it is folded, it wraps around the book in the same way a standard dust jacket.

French fold dust jacket. The top and bottom edges are folded but a standard jacket is trimmed at the edge. The fold over is black in this photo because the jacket background is black.

A French fold jacket is a more elegant style for a high-quality book. The result is that you have a fold on the top and bottom of the French fold jacket. A standard dust jacket is trimmed on top and bottom, having no fold.

A French fold dust jacket is more durable and looks expensive, but is a relatively low-cost option.

Another example of a French fold dust jacket showing both top and bottom fold overs. The background color extends just slightly over the fold over in this photo.

Book dimensions, spine width, page count, and paper thickness will vary among printers. The service provider can provide you with the measurements used for their press and equipment.

This is yet another option that is not supplied by print-on-demand services—and not many book printers—except for Star Print Brokers.

CHAPTER SEVEN | EXTRAS FOR BOOKS

FRENCH FOLD DUST JACKET INDESIGN FILE   SET-UP

Ask provider for French fold dust jacket measurement template.

Follow the set-up for a standard dust jacket. The only difference is adding the top and bottom flap. The height of each flap size depends on the service provider used.

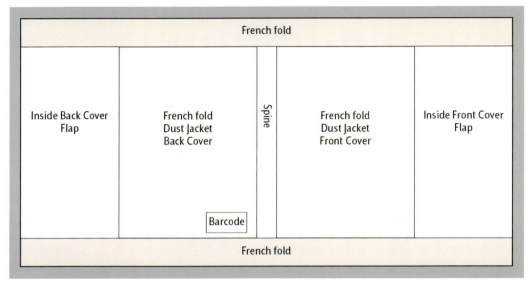

French fold dust jacket set-up

Vellum tip-in sheet

A Tip-in sheet simply means that we are placing the sheet by hand in the book and gluing it in place.

The vellum sheet is translucent, and it is almost always printed with an image or message. The sheet is usually found at the very front of the book, but can be elsewhere.

Translucent tip-in page in a hardcover or soft cover book

Belly band

This is a paper band that wraps around the book. It may be secured to itself or have its ends tucked inside the covers. A belly band is typically printed but can be blank. Design it any way you wish. If it is as tall as the book, it is a *sleeve*.

A belly band will not stay in place, nor will it be in the same place on every book, as it may move, since it is not affixed to the cover.

Consider, too, if the book will be sold in bookstores. Browsers may remove the belly band, thereby spoiling the cover/band effect.

A belly band can also wrap round the front cover, spine, and back cover, leaving the last side open. In this case, the ends of the band would be tucked into the inside front and inside back covers. This better keeps the band in place.

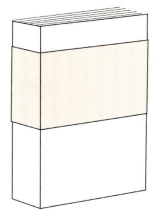

Belly band on a hardcover or soft cover book

Tip-on cover sticker

We discussed the vellum tip-in sheet previously, not to be confused with a tip-*on* sticker. It is placed on the cover wrap of a book that is most often cloth or leather.

A tip-on sticker is an image usually printed in process color on a permanent adhesive backing. A gloss or matte lamination is added giving the sticker a custom look. The 0.125 inch bleed is trimmed off.

The book designer may create a file for a foil or blind stamp with the tip-on sticker. The tip-on sticker can be almost any shape.

Tip-on sticker on a hardbook cover

A tip-on sticker can be put on a slip case too. Options like this cannot be found with print on-demand services.

TIP-ON COVER STICKER INDESIGN FILE SET-UP

The InDesign set-up is simply the exact dimensions of the sticker. Add 0.125 inches or 3 millimeters bleed. If foil stamping is desired, then include a black box about 0.125 inch larger than the size of the sticker, showing where the sticker will be placed.

If there is to be no foil, the printer may also request a separate file with the sticker showing where it will be placed on the cover.

Spot varnish

Imagine printing a book on a coated matte paper. A spot gloss varnish can print over each image. The photos and images appear to "pop" off the pages of the book.

It is also interesting to print spot matte varnish over images printed on gloss paper. The technique is different from a flood varnish. Flood varnish covers the entire page.

You need to add an additional InDesign file to print spot varnish. The spot varnish may be printed on just images, or any large headlines or other graphics images as well.

Do not apply varnish to headlines with small thin type. It requires the use of a different varnish.

Make sure the cost for varnish is included in the quote. It is an additional cost as it adds a fifth tray on a typical 6-color press. Photos print from four trays: Cyan, Magenta, Yellow, and blacK.

SPOT VARNISH INDESIGN FILE   SET-UP

It is easy to make a spot varnish file and apply a spot varnish object style.

1. If varnish is used on images, provide a file that is separate from the native InDesign text file. Although you can create another file layer for the varnish, Star Print Brokers prefers to receive the varnish file as a separate file.
2. First, make a duplicate file of the book and delete anything that should not be varnished.
3. Put selection tool (the first arrow in the Tools palette) on an image to be varnished.
4. Go to (Window > Style > Object styles). Click on three horizontal lies in top right. Select "New Object Style." When the Object Styles panel is open, you will see "Based On," select "[None]."

5. With the New Object Style window open as in the image on the opposite page, under Basic Attributes, check "Fill." Click on "Fill." Make sure the color selected is "Black," and the border is "none."
6. Under Effects in (select Object), check Transparency. It should be the only thing checked.
7. In Style Name, type "Spot Varnish." Effects for "object" will be 100 percent black fill with no border.

Apply Spot Varnish Object Style

Note: The "Selection tool" is the first arrow in the Tools palette in InDesign. The second arrow beneath that is the "Direct Selection tool." Be careful to select the right tool as noted in the instructions.

Page before varnish file is made

Page after the varnish file is made

8. Using the Selection tool, select "Spot Varnish" that you created under Object Styles.
9. Then select the image.
10. With the image still selected, use the second arrow, the "Direct Select tool." You will see the box around the image change, so that there is a dot in each of the four corners. Click the image once and you will still see the four dots, plus four more on the top, bottom, and sides of the image.
11. Do a right-click (or Control-X) and delete the image. A solid black image will remain in the same size and position as the now deleted image.
12. Do not forget to delete the page numbers on this file, which is easy to do if you have set the page numbers set up on master pages.

Foil emboss / stamp

Terminology is important and is often misused when discussing foil embossing. The following are terms to know to enhance the look and feel of a book.

- EMBOSS: To raise a surface. A metal die needs to be created.
- DEBOSS: To depress a surface. A metal die needs to be created.
- STAMP: Depress a surface on the cover.
- BLIND STAMP: Referring to a stamped area where no foil is applied.
- FOIL: Applied to either a stamped or embossed surface.

The most common applications:

- foil embossing of a dust jacket or printed cover wrap
- foil stamp of a cover wrap

Most often a foil emboss (raised) is for a soft cover book or a dust jacket on a hardcover book. Although you can emboss a printed cover on a hardcover book too. Foils come is many colors and even patterns.

A foil stamp (depressed) is used on any surface but is a popular choice for the spine and front cover of hardcover books.

Most of these options cannot be found with POD services. If you really feel that you must go POD, check to see if any of these options are available.

FOIL EMBOSS / STAMP INDESIGN FILE   SET-UP

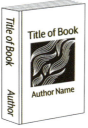

The InDesign file set-up is in black only

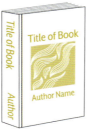

The result is that everything is foiled

FOIL OR BLIND STAMP

After designing the book cover, duplicate the InDesign file showing just the spine and front cover in black. A die is made from the file.

A stamp or a deboss is not often used on the back cover. SPB does not use the standard block letters on the spine that some POD services require. We print or make a die from your file.

The die stamps or burnishes areas on the cover and spine for the book title, author's name, and the area where the tip-on sticker might be applied by hand. The title and author area may be foiled or not foiled, If it has no foil, we call thst a blind stamp instead of a foil stamp.

130   BOOK DESIGN: SIMPLE & PROFESSIONAL

FOIL OR BLIND EMBOSS

Duplicate the file. Remove anything not to be embossed which usually leaves the book title and mayb the author's name. Change the color to black for this die file. Any intricate details cannot be embossed.

Note: Do not confuse the cover wrap with a dust jacket.

Book sleeve

A book sleeve covers the entire cover of the book. It can be printed or left blank. Book sleeves are used for hardcover books, soft cover books, or magazines. A book sleeve can be shorter to show part of an image on a book cover.

A book sleeve covers the front, back, and sides of the book. It may be printed or not.

A sleeve can be embossed, have a foil stamp, a blind stamp, a UV coating, a laminate, or varnish. The stock can be fairly heavy.

A cost consideration is adding any other options or embellishment. We can manufacture a permanent adhesive sticker to seal the sleeve, or as a graphic element.

We would not recommend this for most books. But if you are printing a catalogue, brochure, or inexpensive piece, consider a sleeve. A book needs to have more protection than a book sleeve can provide for mailing.

You need only put a mailing label on the cover and the publication is ready to go. Bear in mind that the United States Postal Service has extremely specific regulations. If you are going to be using a sleeve, check with either the USPS or your local mail house.

They can give you a mailing quote and advise you about regulations. Be prepared with basic specifications. It would be good to get a book and sleeve printing quote first. Then talk to your mail house.

The sleeve can be set up in InDesign. Let us know the dimensions and we will verify so that the sleeve overlaps enough to seal securely. You may want the image or graphics to bleed, that is to print off the trimmed sleeve. If so, add 0.125 inches or 3 millimeters to the top and bottom.

Journal with elastic band

A journal or notebook with an elastic band can be manufactured in so many ways and with so many different options. The elastic is on the back cover, but the reader pulls it over both covers to secure the closed book.

Start by selecting your options for the hardcover book. The book in this photograph is a hardcover with black cloth and black elastic.

Choose the covering material, whether it is cloth, a faux leather, or a printed cover wrap with your own design. The cloth and faux leather come in a variety of colors, as does the elastic band.

You can add a ribbon marker that is the same color as the elastic, but this is optional.

The back cover of a hardcover journal with an elastic band

More options

Hardcover books can be padded. Add a blind stamp. Blind means that the line art, like a logo, is pressed or stamped into the cover.

You can also have a foil stamp. The first thing that comes to mind with self-publishers when they hear the word "foil" is silver or gold foil.
Star Print Brokers can stamp different colors of gold, silver, bronze, rainbow foil, and more. We have foils with patterns. The notebook or journal can be stamped with a matte or gloss foil.

Perhaps you would opt for a black, blue, or red foil stamp. Imagine the cover with your logo or book title in a matte black foil stamp.

Because the journal or notebook is essentially a hardcover book with a thin flexible cover, it will have endpapers. The default stock for endpapers is plain white stock. They can also be printed in color, printed with your design, or a specialty paper may be used. We can even add a pocket on the endpapers inside the front or back cover.

Hardcover endpaper pockets

Gusseted hardcover endpaper pocket

This pocket is placed on the inside back cover of a hardcover book.

Look closely at the photograph to see a gusset made from the same color printed endpaper.

The pocket is placed on the inside front or back cover next to the hinge, so contents put into the pocket will not fall out.

If there is no InDesign file for the endpapers and gusset, you may simply provide the spot PMS ink or process color PMS ink to print.

If there is an InDesign file, set-up the endpaper document as illustrated on page 116 of this chapter. Ask the printer you use for the gusset measurements.

Hardcover endpaper pocket constructed with a gusset

Hook and loop pocket envelope

This is a pocket envelope with a hook and loop closure that allows it to re-close.

In this photograph, it is shown on the inside back cover of a Wire-O hardcover book but could be added to any hardcover or soft cover book.

The pocket size can be adjusted as needed to fit the inside cover or pocket placement.

A hook and loop closure pocket on inside of the book's back cover

PART THREE

Print

- Authentic book printing and binding
- Traditional binding vs. print-on-demand
- Color printing
- Why is the color off?
- Hardcover spines and binding
- Soft cover spines and binding
- ISBN and barcode
- Retail price
- Create the PDF to print on press
- Uploading or sending files

PRINTING ON PRESS
Quality Books

BOOKS ARE TRADITIONALLY PRINTED ON COMMERCIAL OFFSET printing presses and bound in signatures. They can also be output on digital output devices but that is not printing.

It is necessary to understand the differences between spot and process color, RGB compared to CMYK, and press printing vs. print-on-demand. Then there is adding inks to press, selecting paper, bindings, ISBN, barcodes, book pricing, PDFs, and sending files to press. All are covered in this chapter.

 QUICK TIPS

- Hardcover books should always be printed on press as should high quality soft cover books.
- Use Pantone Color Bridge to compare spot ink to process screen-builds, as often they do not look the same when printed.
- Buy the ISBN from ISBN.org, or a seller authorized by ISBN. Otherwise, someone else may be the publisher of your book.

Authentic book printing and binding

Our company prints books on sheet-fed offset presses, printing on large sheets (signatures.) We do not print on web presses which is a press that prints on huge rolls of paper continuously fed to the press. Web press printing is not as accurate as sheet-fed printing. It is for printing newspapers, magazines, or long runs of direct mail—high-quantity but not high-quality.

We do not offer print-on-demand (POD) either. Our printing is excellent, as are our binding materials for our hardcover books. There are many options at our company that are hard to find elsewhere.

Soft cover books with an average spine width is not a bad choice at print-on-demand services, if you need just a few copies. Two-page spreads are a problem. The spread gets clipped in the gutter which will never

Photo by Bank Phrom on Unsplash

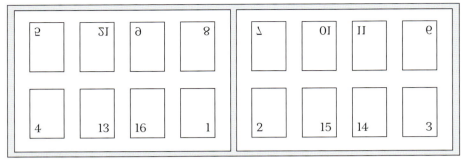

Imposition for 16-page sheet (signature) printing on a commercial printing press

Sheet-fed printing on press.

An output device. There are larger, upgraded devices.

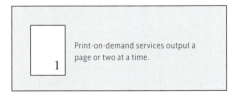

Print-on-demand services output a page or two at a time.

happen when printing on press. It only happens with books that are output. The on-demand problem of toner instead of ink is a problem because toner can smear.

Book printing

We manufacture *high-quality books;* therefore, our books print on sheet-fed presses. Large sheets of paper have 4, 8, 12, or 16 pages printed on both sides.

The sheets are folded three times into signatures. Think of a signature as a booklet. The signatures are bound together to form a book block.

The designer does *not* set-up the imposition to print.

Most process color sheet-fed presses for book printing are 6-color and have six ink trays for inks. Ink is used when printing on press. Print-on-demand books that are digitally output, use toner. The toner can smear when lightly wiped with a moist finger.

138   BOOK DESIGN: SIMPLE & PROFESSIONAL

High-quality or high page count soft cover books should print on press. Output book pages reproduce a page or two at a time, just like from a desktop printer. A book with many pages should print in signatures and be Smyth Sewn so pages do not fall out.

Book binding

The binding of books printed on press can be considered an art. The books are bound after the entire run is printed. However, depending on the printing facility's equipment, soft cover books may be bound at the same time they are printed.

Bound books consist of hardcover, soft cover, Wire-O, spiral, coil, and board books. Wire-O books can be hardcover or soft cover. They can have no spine, or a spine that is semi-concealed, or fully concealed.

Read about the options to become more familiar with them. This might be something to explore with a representative. It is our pleasure to listen to your needs and make suggestions. This is precisely the reason that everything we do is custom manufactured. We have come up with some interesting solutions to book binding problems over the decades.

HARDCOVER

There are binding variations for hardcover books. These include square spine, rounded spine, and hollow spine books. There are also lay-flat books, journals, Wire-O, coil, spiral, and more. The signatures of hardcover books are often Smyth Sewn, especially for higher-page count books. Ours are always Smyth Sewn.

The cover wrap is the material that covers the boards of a hardcover book. Options are cloth such as linen or other fabrics, bonded leather, faux leather, faux cloth, and printed paper. The last is the least costly and very widely used.

All hardcover books have endpapers. They may be printed or not. They are pasted to the inside front and back covers. Dust jackets are the loose printed paper that covers a book. It is optional. There is also the choice of a standard dust jacket or a French fold dust jacket. Both types of dust jackets have flaps that are usually printed with a book summary and author biography and photo.

A book is defined as acase bound if it has endpapers. Sometimes the boards that are used to bind a book are deliberately very thin, to be flexible.

Otherwise, the thickness of the board depends on the number of pages in a book, the book's size and the thickness of the paper.

Cloth covered books most often have foil stamping or a blind stamp on the cover and spine. They may also have tip-on images, a bumper box, and more.

Head and tail bands are added to all the books we print. They are customarilyy added to high-quality books. See in Chapter 7, *Extras for Book*s, page 122.

SOFT COVER

There are options for softcover books as well. The book you are reading is a soft cover book with French flaps. The flaps are an extension of the front and back covers. This book has both flaps. A book may be designed with one flap extended from either the front or back cover. The width of a flap must make sense. If it is too narrow, it has no function. A flap needs to be less than the width of the cover. That is because the flap is scored and then folded behind the cover.

Soft cover books have signatures that may be Smyth Sewn and / or glued together to form the book block.

It is a common option to have the title and author embossed and foiled on the cover and spine of a soft cover book. It is not mandatory. Foil embossing is harder to view on Amazon than it is in a bookstore. If books will be sold in a bookstore where they can easily be compared to other books, the embossed foil title makes a strong impression.

Traditional binding vs. print-on-demand

Binding is incredibly important. Hardcover books bound by book printers are completely different than hardcover binding at a POD provider.

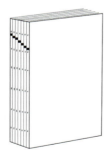

Smyth Sewn signatures with collating marks are often used in traditional hardcover book binding

Side sewn signatures, used in print-on-demand hardcover book binding

140   BOOK DESIGN: SIMPLE & PROFESSIONAL

Print-on-demand providers side-sew or glue single pages. Side-sewn books not only look different, but if there are crossover graphics or a two-page spread, the middle on the image is buried in the gutter.

Traditional printers Smyth Sew books avoiding clipped images and awkward endpaper issues.

Hardcover books have endpapers. If using a traditional printer, ends are the width of two pages. Because of the way POD hardcover books are assembled, the endpapers may be the width of a single page. When this happens, it is because the book block is side-sewn instead of Smyth Sewn.

Color printing

When designing a book with color photographs, illustrations, or type, an understanding of color on the printed page is vital. What you see on your computer screen may not be what you see on the pages of the printed book.

RGB

Red, Green, and Blue are the colors used in RGB. The color is created from colored light. RGB is not only for monitors, but also any screen that reproduces color for television, movies, mobile phones, tablets, laptops, and digital cameras for color photographs.

RGB has the widest array of color but is not used to reproduce photographs and images that print on press. The images need first to be converted to CMYK to print properly.

CMYK

Cyan, **M**agenta, **Y**ellow, and blac**K** are the four inks that make up CMYK

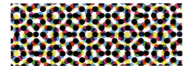

CMYK rosette
Copyright Reamolko on Bigstock

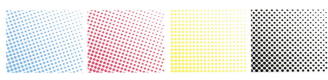

CMYK screen angles
Copyright NonikaStar on Bigstock

process color printing. Process color book printers usually print on 6-color commercial printing presses in CMYK. Sometimes a spot ink or varnish is added, but the cost is extra. CMYK has its issues because of a more limited color array. The designer fine tunes process color to look great on their monitor. Sometimes when the books are printed the color is off. It is usually

CHAPTER EIGHT | PRINTING ON PRESS   141

the designer or the printer who gets the blame. But that might not be the story at all.

While process color images can be at times difficult to get right on press, these are usually problems with viewing color or not understanding spot versus press color results. Self-publishers and designers may need to better understand what happens on press if it is not a proof or press problem.

ROSETTE

Use a loupe, linen tester, or magnifying glass and look at a full-color printed photograph to see the rosette. Screens are reproduced at different angles: Cyan 15°, Magenta 75°, Yellow 0°, and blacK 45°. This produces a rosette, the process color dot pattern seen on closer magnification of a printed image.

Process color

Process color printing uses CMYK, the four inks used on a printing press. As stated previously on the preceding page, it is composed of Cyan, Magenta, Yellow, and blacK. Color photographs are printed in CMYK, never RGB.

Even some mock duotones are printed in process color. Printing is not an exact science, but we can come incredibly close using the right equipment, proofs, and knowledgeable staff.

CMYK Process Color

Getting great color is a process. What we do, and the advice we give varies. Some authors want "pleasing color" which is our standard. Others may need "exact match" which costs more to achieve because of the cost of additional proofs.

"Exact match" means generating press proofs or wet proofs. Since printing is an art, even exact match may not match precisely on every page of every book.

142   BOOK DESIGN: SIMPLE & PROFESSIONAL

Spot color

One ink tray on a press filled with a pre-mixed ink prints a spot color. In addition to knowing what these terms mean, book designers also need to know how to designate color correctly in InDesign. Spot color is one ink added to a tray on a printing press. Sometimes a PMS ink is selected. If only one spot ink is in use on press, images and text will all print in that color.

Spot ink

Spot color in red for Coca-Cola
Photo by Laura Chouette on Unsplash

Two or three spot color inks can certainly be used on press. Usually when more than four spot color inks, it is more cost effective to use process color. The exception is if you have a logo color that does not reproduce well in process color. You need to print that in spot. If you compare the same spot color next to process color inks, the printed result may be quite different.

The Coca-Cola brand has been around since 1886. The beverage manufacturer has their own formula to print Coca-Cola red. If we match this *spot* ink color exactly and compare it to a *process 4-color screenbuild in CMYK*, it will not match. This is a perfect example of CMYK having a narrower color array than RGB. The solution for a brand like Coca-Cola, or even a color in a book that does not look the same when viewed in process color, is to use a spot color. That always means adding another ink tray to the press.

Adding inks on press

The Pantone Library is practically indispensable. It can be pricey for new designers. If you can only buy just one swatch book or fan deck, buy the Pantone Color Bridge. The reason is that it has the process color screenbuild (CMYK) and the solid (SPOT) inks side-by-side. It also has the HTML color equivalent.

The Pantone swatch deck may be used to evaluate color choices. Even if you are choosing CMYK colors in InDesign or Photoshop swatches, the best and most cost-effective way to have full control over color is to select screen builds from the Pantone Color Bridge. Adding a fifth color on press costs more. Check with your printer *before* you set-up your InDesign files.

Why is the color off?

As discussed in Chapter 2, *Planning a Book* on pages 43 to 44, CMYK process color will not always look the same as RGB, because RGB is made up of three lights: Red, Green, and Blue. It is meant for viewing on digital devices.

Process color is made up of the four inks used in color printing: Cyan, Magenta, Yellow, and blacK. These are the inks used to print color photographs on commercial printing presses. This offers a narrower color array than RGB. While we would love to have RGB color in books, it is not possible unless we put a monitor on every page.

The good news is that software technology in general, and monitors have improved in recent years. "Pleasing color" or even "exact match" color is easier to achieve, but not always possible. Do not blame the designer or printer quite yet! There are a few things that you need to know to be realistic about color. Sometimes our expectations must be adjusted.

When RGB images are converted to CMYK, you may see color shift on the screen as you convert the images in Photoshop. Most of the time, please use the *U.S. Sheetfed Coated v2* destination space profile for Star Print Brokers. Other printers may use a different profile. While we can convert images for you, we ask the self-publisher or book designer to do the conversion, so the shift can be seen with one's own eyes on one's own monitor.

Most often, the greatest color shift is in the blues, especially blue skies. It also happens in hot pink. However, we did an entire photography book with fuchsia flowers and they all turned out perfectly. This shift in color may also show up more in metallic colors.

If you see a digitally output proof, the color may not be exact. A lot of that has to do with the output device. One round, a full set of physical digitally output proofs is included in every quote we do. However, some may want a press proof or wet proof to see exact match. This is quite costly and usually not necessary.

Book printing is an art, not a science. The average person does not see color with the very keen eye of a photographer, fine artist, or top graphic designer. While we usually please even the fussiest, we cannot please everyone all of the time. Printing a book is not like printing one poster 50,000 times. There are many color pages in coffee table books. We can print pleasing color or exact match. But not even the finest printers guarantee perfect color on every page of every book. Additionally, each individual perceives color in their own unique way.

Variations in color

Please use default Adobe InDesign settings unless we advise a change. Don't use any SWOP profile, as it is for web presses. Star Print Brokers prints on sheet fed presses. Web presses use huge rolls of paper, usually to print newspapers or magazines.

PRINTED COLOR

When viewing any printed color, standardized lighting conditions are critical, using daylight lighting, 5000 K lamps. The International Standards Organization established ISO 3664:2009. When viewing printed images, a light source replicating D50 light should be used. That is not realistic for most readers.

MONITOR AND SCREEN COLOR

When viewing color on a computer monitor, laptop, iPad, iPhone, or any digital screen or monitor, it must be realized that the viewing device may not be color-calibrated correctly or calibrated at all. Additionally, the lighting conditions are almost never the standardized ISO 3664:2009.

ABOUT DESTINATION SPACE PROFILES AND ICC PROFILES

Our printers moved away from using ICC profiles in recent years, but POD providers use them as they output pages on digital output devices.

We ask clients to use the Destination space profile (File > Convert to Profile) *U.S. Sheetfed Coated v2* or *U.S. Sheetfed Uncoated v2*. An ICC profile is not needed, but we can provide one if they insist. Each image is ready for press when converted to CMYK using one of the above profiles.

- Star Print Brokers can convert your images as described above.
- POD vendors can give you an ICC profile for their specific output devices.
- Other printers may give you a profile that is different than what we would specify.

Know the paper stock finish when selecting inks

Will you use coated or uncoated stock? Most authors prefer coated stock, especially for coffee table books. The interior pages of a hardcover book are usually printed on coated stock, but not always.

BOOK INTERIOR AND COVER | COLOR PRINTING SET-UP

Coated or Uncoated paper

There are different InDesign library options to select from in the Swatches palette. Go to Swatches and select "New Color Swatch" from the pull-down menu and choose your option.

Spot color setup

COLOR TYPE: Spot

COLOR MODE: Pantone + Solid Coated or Pantone + Solid Uncoated depending on the paper stock used.

Process color, CMYK setup

COLOR TYPE: Process

COLOR MODE: CMYK or other Pantone libraries.

Example: Pantone + Color Bridge Coated for coated stock.

Example: Pantone + Color Bridge Uncoated for uncoated stock.

Example: CMYK if you are picking a color out of a photograph with the eyedropper tool.

We use the library for coated or uncoated stock depending on the stock being used. I also use the Pantone Color Bridge color modes in conjunction with physical Pantone Color Bridge fan decks.

ENDPAPERS | COLOR PRINTING SET-UP

Uncoated paper

Go to Swatches and select "New Color Swatch" from the pull-down menu and choose your option.

Scenario: A self-publisher wants nice, deep black endpapers. They do *not* want the endpapers to print in spot black, using 100 percent black. To achieve the deeper black, either spot or process may be used. The endpaper examples are for *uncoated endpapers* which are standard.

Spot color setup

COLOR TYPE: Spot

COLOR MODE: Select Pantone + Color Solid Uncoated on the pull-down menu. Scroll to the bottom of the color list to find black inks. Select one, choosing from Pantone Black 2 U through U7. U = Uncoated

Process color, CMYK setup

COLOR TYPE: Process

COLOR MODE: While you can select CMYK, you might also select Pantone + Color Bridge Uncoated from the pull-down menu.
Scroll to the bottom of the color list to find black inks. Select one, choosing from Pantone Black 2 U through U 7.
UP = Uncoated Process

You can also use these instructions to set any other ink choices in spot or process inks on uncoated stock. We call our uncoated paper "Woodfree."

Hardcover spines and bindings

For hardcover books, spines may be square (flat) or round.

Most often Star Print Brokers will Smyth Sew the text block of hardcover and soft cover books. Smyth Sewing is not needed for Wire-O bindings.

Square spine

The square spine may be tight, or it may be hollow.

A tight square spine for a hardcover binding

TIGHT SQUARE SPINE

With a tight square spine, the book block is securely glued to the board of the spine.

HOLLOW SQUARE SPINE

The book block of a hollow square spine is not glued to the board of the spine.

The hollow square spine makes the book block more flexible with better lay-flat performance, but it is not as strong as a tight square spine.

This is a hollow square spine for a hardcover binding

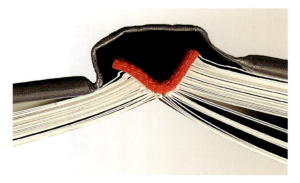

A round spine hardcover is hollow and has no spine board

Round spine

A round spine hardcover is always hollow and has no spine board. The round spine is the most flexible with the best lay-flat performance. However, the disadvantage is less strength especially for books with larger page counts.

Hardcover Wire-O

OPEN

No photograph is provided here.
This book binding has no spine at all. The draw back for self-publishers is that it does not have a spine. Most bookstores will not carry it.

Round back Wire-O hardcover binding

CONCEALED ROUND SPINE

The wire is completely concealed in a rounded spine. It is great for high page count books that need to lay flat.

CONCEALED

This is a great lay-flat Wire-O binding. The wire is totally concealed. The title of the book on the spine is visible just as it is with any other hardcover book.

SEMI-CONCEALED ON THE SPINE

No photo is provided here.
We seldom bind Wire-O books with wire exposed on the spine.

Concealed Wire-O hardcover binding

BOOK DESIGN: SIMPLE & PROFESSIONAL

The reason is that the wire partially obstructs the spine, making it unsuitable for printing.

The semi-concealed Wire-O on back cover next to the spine of a hardcover book is more attractive, stronger, and less conspicuous.

SEMI-CONCEALED ON THE BACK COVER

This binding is a great solution when you need the strength of a Wire-O binding combined with the wire exposure being less not readable as it is on the back cover.

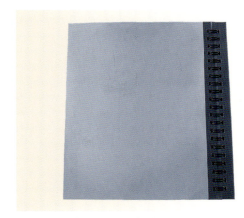

A semi-concealed hardcover Wire-O on back cover next to the spine.

Another benefit is that bookstores will not reject the book because of its binding. They usually will not accept books with no spine, or a wire obstructing the spine. The semi-concealed Wire-O on the back cover is the best choice for higher or heavier page counts.

Soft cover spines and bindings

For soft cover books, spines are square (flat). Star Print Brokers will usually Smyth Sew the text block of soft cover as well as hardcover books. Sewing is never applicable to Wire-O bindings.

Smyth Sewn

This is the highest quality binding for a soft cover book. The printed signatures are Smyth Sewn just as with Star Print Brokers' high-quality hardcover books. The text block is then glued into the soft cover case. PUR glue may also be used for even added flexibility. The binding is very strong and offers the best near lay-flat performance for a soft cover book unless going to Wire-O for completely lay flat performance.

Perfect bound

The bindery will "rough up" and glue on the cover for a perfect bound book. A 'perfect binding' is the lowest cost option. It works well for novels with an average to small page count. If the book has a higher page count, we advise a more secure binding style, like a notch or burst binding.

Variations of Perfect Bindings:

PUR GLUE (POLYURETHANE REACTIVE)

Do you need extra strength and flexibility? Use PUR glue with a perfect binding. Many authors need the more lay-flat performance of a PUR glue perfect binding.

NOTCH BOUND

The spine has notches and glue. A soft cover book may be notch bound. Small notches are cut out of the spine side of the signatures. Glue fills in the notches and then the cover is applied.

BURST BOUND

The spine has perforations and is glued. It is more durable than a simple perfect binding. Notch and burst bound are just variations on a theme.

Soft cover Wire-O

OPEN

This book binding has no spine at all. The draw back for self-publishers is that there is no spine. Most bookstores will not carry it.

CONCEALED SPINE

The wire is completely concealed by a square spine. It is great for higher page count books that need to lay flat.

SEMI-CONCEALED ON SPINE

We rarely bind Wire-O books with wire on the spine. The reason is that the wire partially obstructs the spine making it unprintable. The semi-concealed Wire-O on the back cover next to the spine is more attractive and less conspicuous.

SEMI-CONCEALED ON BACK COVER

This binding is a great solution when you need the lay-flat performance of a Wire-O binding combined with the wire being out of the way as it is attached to the back cover. Another benefit is that bookstores will not reject the book because of the binding.

Lamination for all books

A printed cover, cover wrap, or dust jacket needs extra protection. Some providers apply a UV coating or a varnish to these surfaces. Star Print Brokers applies a lamination which is far more durable. It is a permanent surface that will not lift up.

None of these surfaces will protect a book from direct sunlight. They do offer some protection from scuffs and wear and tear. The cost is automatically included in our quotes. The client need only decide if they prefer matte or gloss lamination. Soft touch lamination is available at an additional cost.

When designing a cover, a cover wrap, or dust jacket, know that fingerprints may show, even with any varnish or lamination. If there are larger areas where no image or text are apparent, consider using a subtle texture in the design. It makes any fingerprints of scuffs less noticeable.

MATTE LAMINATION

This lamination provides a softer look with no shine. Matte lamination is what we use for most of our books, but it is really a matter of personal choice. Also, a gloss UV coating can be applied on large type or an image to give the cover even more visual impact.

GLOSS LAMINATION

A high-gloss look is what this lamination provides. It also tends to show more fingerprints. A matte UV coating can be applied on large type or an image to give the cover an exciting look.

SOFT TOUCH LAMINATION

This is a relatively new finish. Matte soft touch adds a little to the cost but has a very luxurious look and wonderful feel.

If a book is to be sold online only, the buyer will not be able to see the finish of the lamination. However, if the book will be sold in bookstores or in person, Soft touch lamination creates a great first impression.

Create the PDF to print on press

PDFs need to be set up correctly or the client will be advised to remake them. To create PDFs in Adobe InDesign go to File > Export . . . to desktop or folder > click Save. Save PDFs to the desktop or in the folder for a book in progress.

HELPFUL HINTS:

- When first setting up a book file in InDesign, make sure to check 'Facing Pages'. Go to File > Document Setup . . . This places the first page in a right-hand page position and it is numbered page 1. The following pages are in two-page spreads. A book always has an even number of pages. The last page in a book is a left-hand page that has an even number.
- The crop marks, bleed marks, and color bars are generated when creating a PDF. They are not made in the InDesign file.

Years ago, printers asked to have native files (in this case, InDesign files) sent to prepress. However, technology has changed for the better. The finest books are printed from properly prepared PDFs. Printers seldom print from InDesign files any longer. Printing from an InDesign file is now the exception.

The following is a reference guide to make PDF files to print books, specifically with Star Print Brokers.

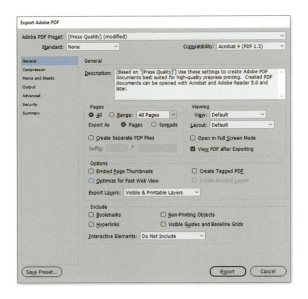

GENERAL TAB

- Left column: General tab
- Adobe PDF Preset: Choose **Press Quality** because "Print Quality" is meant for output to desktop printers, not printing on press.
- Compatibility: Acrobat 4 (PDF 1.3). Once this option is selected, Press Quality becomes "Press Quality (modified)." Acrobat 5 and higher have functions not needed to print on press, like preserving linkable text. Acrobat 5 and higher can interfere with imposition software that printer's use to prepare files for printing.

MARKS AND BLEEDS TAB

- Left column: Marks and Bleeds tab.
- "Spreads" box *un*checked. PDFs in single pages, NOT spreads.
- Under "Marks", check the box: All Printer's Marks.
- Below that, check box: Use Document Bleed Settings. If you have set the bleed correctly in the Document Setup, you will see 0.125 in each box. It is also okay to have the inside box set to zero.

OUTPUT TAB

- Left column: Output tab. Use the default settings. If you no longer have default settings, please use the following.
- Color Conversion: "Convert to Destination (Preserve Numbers)".
- Profile Inclusion Policy: Select "Don't Include Profiles."
- Click "Export" to make PDF files. Your PDF will automatically open.

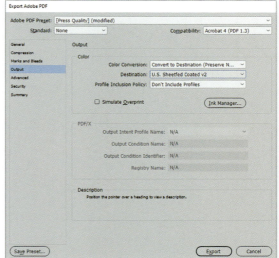

Uploading or sending files

The PDF files may be placed on the providers' FTP site or uploaded to DropBox. Contact provider for FTP credentials. Email smaller PDFs.

PDFs need all printer's marks and use document bleed settings. The interior pages should be sent in one PDF or chapters can be in one folder. But to print correctly, the book needs to be in single pages, not spreads.

Each of the other components should be in separate file folders. Other PDFs or files could be the cover, cover wrap, dust jacket, endpapers, spot varnish file, foil stamp. It all depends on the binding style and printing customization you choose.

PART FOUR

Sell

- Branding considerations
- The package deals
- Pricing strategy
- Amazon
- Fulfillment
- Distribution
- Social media

SELLING & MARKETING
Sales for Authors

YOUR FIRST BOOK IS WRITTEN and now you are wondering how to print it. While our choice is clear—meaning to print your books with Star Print Brokers—that might not be the first choice for everyone. That is because we print only high-quality books on press, so we have low unit costs but our minimum is 1,000 copies.

 QUICK TIPS

- Be skeptical of package deals. Consider the cost of each service. Is it really a service you would pay for or that you need? What is the cost per book?
- Look beyond the suggestion of distribution. Can a service really get your book into brick-and-mortar bookstores?
- Make sure that you are not being paid only a modest royalty. Keep 100 percent of your profit. Buy the ISBN yourself, so that you are the publisher of your book.
- Build a brand, even if it is only a logo, colors, and typefaces. The other especially important element is to define the image to project to the world.
- Visit a physical bookstore as well as Amazon to help you to develop a pricing strategy.
- Sell books on Amazon because they have the most traffic.
- Print with Star Print Brokers because they print the best books.

The package deals

Read all details before committing to work with any printer, print-on-demand service, or publisher. Do not sign any contract unless you thoroughly understand it. Our suggestion is to not sign away your rights. You may wish to consult your own attorney.

HOW MUCH FOR DOES 1 TO 50 OR SO BOOKS REALLY COST?

Authors can print a handful of books but watch out for the package deals as you may end up paying thousands of dollars for very few books. Some providers have package deals, and they may also sell services à la carte. These are often services that are not really services at all, or you can buy them yourself for a lot less.

Package deal services may include things such as: "printing" which for a few books is invariably not printing on press, but outputting your file on a digital output device like a higher-end desktop printer, manuscript evaluation, royalties, cover lamination, availability to bookstores, author support, volume discounts, a press release, and more.

An important question is: "Why would you pay thousands of dollars to get a royalty when you can keep 100 percent of the profit with Star Print Brokers or printing on your own?" Are they saying that a royalty is all of the profit, or is it a lot less because you are getting paid a modest royalty minus additional services costs?

If one of the top publishers wants to publish your book and pay royalties, that is something to consider. But, if you come across a package deal, go to a straight POD provider, your local copy office, print shop, or Star Print Brokers.

You can publish your book yourself for a lot less than most package deals charge. If an author is going to print only a few books, they can also output a few books at a local printshop or copy center. When you are ready for truly high-quality books, print with Star Print Brokers as we provide the highest quality books anywhere. Sell on Amazon because they have the most web traffic anywhere.

Distribution is not offered for brick and mortar bookstores. All you get is availability, which you have anyway when you buy your own ISBN and barcode. Read more about distribution on pages 164 to 165 in this chapter.

ROYALTIES

Why? If you buy an ISBN and barcode at ISBN.org, you are the publisher of your book and retain all profit. If anyone offers you a free ISBN and barcode, they will become the publisher and you will receive only royalties.

When you buy an ISBN at ISBN.org, you will receive a Publisher Record Number which identifies your account with your specific account number. You can access this account.

Think about it. One ISBN and barcode costs around $150. Why would a publisher pay that much if they weren't going to make that much back, or be charging that much more in their package deal?

Star Print Brokers can also sell one ISBN and barcode because we are an authorized agent of ISBN, but we will also provide you with your own Publisher Record Number as supplied by ISBN. If you do not get an account number at ISBN, you are probably not the publisher of your book.

Branding considerations

A logo is only one aspect of branding. Are you branding your book, yourself as an author, a book designer, or all three? Decide for what or whom you want to develop a brand.

What do you wish the brand to communicate and how should the brand be seen? While it sounds like a daunting task for the novice or non-designer, there are certain things that anyone can do to establish a brand on which to build. Branding is integral to marketing.

A brand is a logo, specific colors, typefaces, a mission statement, the image projected to the world. Who are your clients and what do they expect from your brand? A brand may include a tag line on your website. Correct use of typography, color, and images are important to develop. The brand may be applied to the book, on a website, and on marketing materials.

BOOK BRANDING

Even when writing and selling one title, self-publishers present a better image to potential buyers if the brand is defined. It matters more if you write a series of similar books. Do you write romance novels, horror, or thrillers? You may use the same illustrator or same typefaces, only changing the colors.

However, individual titles should not look the same. Establish which elements can be similar. If you also write in another genre, a poetry book for instance, that should look nothing like your horror book title!

PUBLISHER BRANDING

When becoming a publisher, the individual book title brands have previously been left to the authors or self-publishers that you would now represent.

As a publisher, you create a fully branded website to sell book titles that you represent. The image you project for yourself is that of publisher. It is an uphill climb to promote books on your website or have an online bookstore.

You would have to develop traffic which can take a very long time and may be quite expensive. Why do that when you can link to Amazon?

But, as a publisher, you can, of course, set up an online bookstore. However, if you do not have images that link to Amazon, you will need an eCommerce store to stock and fulfill the books yourself. While it is quite doable, where is the web traffic going to come from? This is why we suggest using Amazon to sell books.

AUTHOR BRANDING

If you are—or plan to become—a prolific writer, build an author website. It may be quite simple, having one page, or just a few. The elements on an author website should dovetail with a book title. These would definitely be the author photo and perhaps colors and typography.

You are selling yourself and promoting your image with marketing materials and a website. As an author, you are going to sell your books. Selling on your site and / or linking to Amazon is your choice.

We work with quite a few authors who have their own built-in network of potential book buyers. You might not need Amazon at all if you are so fortunate as to have your own established network.

Whatever you create for your books, author, or publisher site, will help you to better market your brand if you develop and adhere to branding principles you establish. Answer this question; what makes you unique?

The brand book

Brand books are created by art directors, advertising agencies, and graphic designers to specifically detail all branding elements. It is not a must have unless you have a substantial company, but it never hurts to present a more polished look!

Brand books that are for sale will not be all inclusive, providing book, website, and other types of projects, but you can get some great ideas. Graphic design packages for brand books can be found on some of the many websites that sell graphics. You can buy a brand book for a modest cost. Adobe InDesign, Photoshop, and Illustrator files are provided in the purchase.

Changing a color or typeface might be all that is needed. Then, you can roll the brand book elements out to your book, author or publisher website, and marketing materials.

Pricing strategy

Most of your sales will come from Amazon, unless you have an existing website following. This means that you must allow enough room in your retail price for discounts and other fees.

Start by making a visit to a major bookstore. Gather some books that have subject matter similar to your book. You want to look at competitors! Check the copyright or the printing year if it is listed. The copyright should follow the title page. You need to make sure you are backing into the retail price of your book using a recently printed book and not a title printed ten years ago when costs were lower.

Having a closer look at competitive books is a good exercise to finalize the style of the book that you are writing and / or designing.

Look closely at books of similar dimensions and page count to the book you are printing. Is it hardcover or soft cover? Color throughout or black and white? What special features or options does the book have? The thing you will not know is how many copies were printed. The more copies you print, the lower the unit cost.

Also found on the copyright page is the country where the book was printed. Star Print Brokers has been printing in Asia for over twenty years. We never print in China. Because we print many titles, we get lower pricing and have found the quality of the books is always higher than what is usual in the U.S.A. We also find the service to be superior.

Because we are printing brokers, our unit cost is always lower. We have a handful of select printers that we use. As in every country, there are great printers and there are poor printers. We have never met a printer yet who would not say that they are wonderful, but the test comes when something goes wrong.

How will a problem be handled? That is the core of what we offer to self-publishers and small publishers. We have many references for prospective clients to call and verify our printing services and customer service.

As a side note, we would rather print in the U.S.A., but with higher costs and lower quality, it does not make sense. If that ever changes, we will certainly have another look.

One of the other challenges is all the options we can provide when printing with our current overseas partners. The options are just not available with most printers in the U.S.

Many self-publishers start with printing the minimum which is 1,000 hardcover or 2,000 soft cover books. We are one of the few places that prints board books. Our minimum for board books is 1,000 copies.

Quantity is important to know when planning your retail price. A small publisher may typically print 5,000 or 6,000 copies, particularly on a second printing. Their unit cost is less than a self-publisher starting out with the minimum print run. If they hired a designer for the initial print run, the design cost will not be repeated in a second printing.

After noting the differences and similarities between your new book and existing titles in the bookstore, know that dimensions, page count, binding style, and printing quantity are the big drivers in a retail price.

When you request a quote from Star Print Brokers, please feel free to request a quote for a larger quantities too, like 5,000 or 6,000 copies. We realize you need to plan for future runs as well.

Amazon

Amazon is likely the best bet to sell your book, unless you have an existing fan or following base. The number of people you reach to sell your book is a critical factor.

Let's look at Amazon's numbers. According to Statista, in the December 2018 time period, Amazon had 206.1 million daily visitors. Macy's was at 46.1 million daily. Amazon is by far the most popular retail site.

However, there is a problem with selling your book on Amazon. Since they are so big, it is not easy to be found. We have seen this with books we printed for self-publishers. Some take off and sell thousands of books in the first month. They are the exception, but some of the self-publishers that we work with have been remarkably successful.

First, before you start to write, create a book, author, website, or publishing company, the goal is to start collecting email addresses so you can notify subscribers when your book is released. Build an audience by blogging frequently. Send out your new blogs via email. Each of the blog posts can be a topic to include in your book.

SET A HIGHER RETAIL PRICE TO SELL ON AMAZON

Amazon will discount books to about a third less than the listed retail price. They charge around fifteen percent just to list a title. Add the "look inside" option, as it is money well spent. This feature will bring more sales because people get to look at a few inside pages. Buyers may be making their buying decision from the few pages they see, so choose the pages wisely.

A SUCCESS STORY

We work with a self-publisher who has unique subject matter for her book. The book was released a number of years ago at the beginning of the "autoimmune" and "paleo" interest in this country. Those particular keywords and a few other similar keywords drove sales.

At one point in the first few weeks, the book was ranked 189 in all of Amazon books, and number one in several book categories. It was wonderful to follow the success of this title and do many more print runs.

OTHER ONLINE BOOKSTORES

You can read about on-demand book providers who start an online bookstore to augment their on-demand offerings. They would be lucky to get 1,000 or even 10,000 visitors a day to their store, let alone hundreds of millions of daily visitors. It does not matter if they offer more profit to self-publishers. If the book cannot be found because their bookstore audience is too small, then you are wasting your time.

Star Print Brokers also looked at starting an online bookstore on our website. If it made sense to do so, we would start a store in a heartbeat.

Fulfillment

You can have all or part of your book shipment sent to a local provider. We have used direct mailing services before. Just make sure they have a secure, climate-controlled storage area on site. You are charged for storing the books, shipping them out individually or in batches, and the package or box that is used for shipping, plus postage or other shipping costs.

AMAZON

Amazon will charge around another fifteen percent send to your book to the buyer. The cost of doing business is going up. With the feedback that we get from the self-publishers that we work with, we suggest that you fulfill the first print run yourself. Not only do you save the money that you would have to pay Amazon, but you also get a feel for how quickly or slowly the book moves. If you are printing 3,000 copies or more, fulfillment at Amazon is a reasonable option.

FULFILLMENT AND DIRECT MAIL SERVICES

You can have all or part of your book shipment sent to a local direct mail service provider. There are also fulfillment services, but there is usually a number of direct mailers in suburban and metro areas.

Direct mailers must have a secure, climate-controlled storage area onsite. Self-publishers are charged for storing books, mailing individually or in batches, and the package or box that is used for mailing. Postage is extra.

If self-publishers sell books on their website, add another cost for shipping and handling in addition to the retail price.

Distribution

BOOKSTORE DISTRIBUTION

Have you been lured by headlines touting global book distribution or availability in bookstores? There are companies that provide book distribution, but it is not free, and not inexpensive. Sometimes they insist on printing your book, which can be disastrous for books that need to be high-quality and finely bound. Ask for samples so that you can see the quality.

Here is the secret: **If you buy an ISBN at ISBN.org, your book title is in the database used by all brick and mortar bookstores. You are not being promised anything you do not already have.**

Anyone that offers distribution is unlikely to get your book into physical bookstores. I say unlikely, because they will gladly sell you a display advertisement for several hundred dollars in a quarterly catalogue sent to bookstores. That might get you noticed but does not mean your book will get picked up. The best thing to do is go directly to bookstores with your book in hand and a good sales pitch.

The more successful authors have an Amazon Author page and they target keywords that buyers may search to find a book such as theirs. List in several Amazon book categories and use their "look inside" feature. Book buyers are more likely to buy a book if they can sample a few pages before buying. List your book on Barnes & Noble. Many self-publishers that we have worked with for over two decades follow this formula.

What drives book sales is being found in searches. To be found, you need to be visible. To be visible, you need to not only be part of the large crowd that shops for books on Amazon, but you need to have keywords and information that potential book buyers are looking for.

- Listing on Amazon does not guarantee sales.
- Your own website traffic will boost sales, provided that you already have significant traffic.
- Social Media is a factor in success but only if you put in a great deal of effort and often.
- Even if you already have a built-in network, concentrate on a well-designed book to attract attention.
- Have an Amazon Author page and utilize keywords and phrases. List in several categories.
- Do keyword research for Amazon and your website, so that you know what potential buyers are searching for. Investigate what successful competitors are doing on Amazon and on their websites.

Delivery and shipping costs

The books that Star Print Brokers prints are delivered DDP to the door. The cost is included in ballpark quotes as well as detailed quotes.

Typically, delivery to the door is not included with USA printing quotes. This means that the self-publisher picks up the books themselves or delivery is an extra cost. Get a cost quote for shipping when you get a quote. Listed below are standard shipping and delivery terms and what they mean for self-publishers:

FOB (FREE ON BOARD)

Self-publisher will pay more and have work to do. If the quote is from a USA printer, make sure they provide delivery as well, unless you want to pick up the books at the printer. If it is not clearly stated on the quote, assume delivery is not included.

Lower cost book printing quotes could turn out to be the highest—and mark extra work and expense for self-publishers.

USA: The books are left on the printer's loading dock. The self-publisher needs to arrange for pick up of their books at the printer and delivery to the location where the books will be stored or fulfilled.

Overseas: Books are delivered on board a vessel designated by the self-publisher. The printer fulfills their obligation to deliver when the goods have passed over the ship's rail. The receiver pays inbound customs clearance costs for ocean shipping, and either picks up the books at port, or hires a trucker to pick up and deliver to the final destination.

CIF (COST INSURANCE FREIGHT)

The printer arranges ocean shipping to the port of entry and provides the buyer with the documents necessary to pick up the shipment at port. The recipient is responsible for all inbound customs clearance and delivery arrangements and costs.

DDP (DELIVERED DUTY PAID)

All usual shipping and delivery costs, including the cost of ocean shipping, customs clearance, and delivery to the door are included. GST / VAT (non-U.S. deliveries) are the responsibility of the buyer and are not included. The shipment is insured from departure to delivery by a local trucker.

DDP quotes are all-in. The shipment is delivered to the door, whether that is the front door, garage door of your residence, a storage facility, a mail or fulfillment house, Amazon warehouse, etc. Inside delivery is extra.

Compare book delivery costs on printing quotes. Most buyers choose DDP terms since nearly everything is included except taking the shipment past the threshold of the door.

Social media

Having a social media presence can be a boost to the author, their book(s), a small publisher, or a book designer. It takes time, effort, and knowledge about social media. The more time spent on Facebook, Instagram, Twitter, and Pinterest, the more traffic you will generate. But it takes time to grow.

While Star Print Brokers has over 50,000 Twitter followers, we do not get a lot of clicks. All Tweets have an image, post link, and hashtags.

It is not how many people you follow that is important, but how many follow you on each social media account. Followers are good for Search Engine Optimization (SEO). The question is—where is your time best spent? Is it working on SEO for your website or on Amazon, or on social media?

Establish Social Media Accounts

There is much free and paid information available on how to set-up and post to social media. Find additional instructions on each platform, YouTube, webinars, courses, and links to classes. There are also plenty of graphics that are specific to each platform. Set up accounts for each of these platforms.

FACEBOOK

Log into your personal Facebook account. Select "Create Page." This may be in different locations depending on the device that you are using. Select "Business/Brand" and choose a category. Get instructions to create a Facebook page at this Facebook link: **https://www.facebook.com/business/learn/lessons/tips-to-creating-a-facebook-page**

PINTEREST BUSINESS PAGE

Visit the link below for complete instructions. You will fill in your email address, password, business name, type of business, and website URL. **https://help.pinterest.com/en/business/article/get-a-business-account** You can then follow 5 topics. This is less important if you use Pinterest to promote your brand. Create boards and pins to post.

TWITTER

Use your personal Twitter profile or create a new profile. Go to: **https://help.twitter.com/en/using-twitter/create-twitter-account** for complete instructions. If using your personal profile or a new profile, be sure to add your website information to your bio.

INSTAGRAM

Download the Instagram App, create a profile and add a photo. You can convert a basic profile into a business profile. Post photos and/or videos. Find people to follow and engage with others. Get started here: **https://business.instagram.com/getting-started**

Need to know

A cover image is the background image at the top of your social media page. Each platform has different size requirements. Verify image sizes before creating it. The sizes also vary for **profile photos and bios** on each platform. Always add links to your website or blog.

Consistency

Develop a brand and an overall look for all your sales and marketing efforts. Follow this through on your website and social media. Maintain consistency by having an identifiable brand everywhere.

Marketing

It takes a significant amount of time to market books. Once the book is written and printed, self-publishers can be successful by devoting a few hours a day to marketing their book.

Self-publishers can do their own marketing, hire a book marketer, or depend on marketing services purchased in a "package deal". Small publishers expect authors to do much of their own social media. Publishers have a limited marketing budget for any book. The budget is not extended unless the book is highly successful.

IT IS ALWAYS THE AMOUNT OF TRAFFIC THAT COUNTS THE MOST

There are hundreds of free and paid providers who will promote books through their sites, tweets, etc. **Check their website or social media traffic numbers.** Some have less traffic than our site, but they charge to Tweet, or charge to let you on to their website. This probably does not help you.

The majority of our followers are book-related, and we tweet several times a day. Is it worth it to pay for tweeting your book title? I am not convinced unless they have a much larger list of followers; more than our 50,000 Twitter followers. Also, we do not offer a social media service as there are tons available. We print and design books, and we strive to do both exceedingly well.

Know your niche

Self-publishers most often write about what they know, as they should. They may write several books and these are easier to market if they all fall into the same category. For instance, marketing two or three cookbooks is easier than a novel, a photography book, and a children's book. That is simply because the target audience remains much the same, instead of having to expend three times the effort to market to three different groups.

Build a brand with multiple titles. Building the audience for your first book makes marketing easier for your second book in the same niche.

Laying the foundation

Once your book is written, have the rest of the marketing tools in place to market the book effectively. Know who your audience is. It can be helpful to write a paragraph or two about your target market. What are their demographics? Do they live or recreate locally, regionally or nationally, or globally? What are their interests and hobbies? Are you writing books about fly fishing, gardening, or children's books?

If the last, what age are the children? You can see how defining this information will lead you into planning the target audience to reach on Facebook or other sites, where to send press releases, and the businesses to friend on social media.

BOOK, AUTHOR, PUBLISHER. WHO ARE YOU?

Consider your target market and future plans for your books and your business. Are you selling yourself as as author? Then, you would have a website promoting yourself, as well as the book or books that you are writing. Your domain name might be your name or pen name.

Do you have your own publishing company or business name? The domain name for your website could be the name under which you are publishing.

Here is what you need to have in place:

- Website with a sign-up form for email subscribers.
- Sign up with MailChimp or a provider of your choice to collect sign-ups for your email list. Set up the email or newsletter with your logo.
- An Amazon page to sell the books.
- Authentic book reviews on your Amazon page are helpful selling tools.
- Write a press release and send it out to a list of potential media outlets, bookstores, publications, websites, or qualified email addresses.
- Send an email to your list about your new book launch. Be sure to add a link to Amazon, or where you are selling it.
- Talk to bookstores about carrying your book. This is great for local events, history, etc.
- When something is successful, keep doing it! In anything that you try whether it be advertising or your marketing efforts, never give up after the first try. Of course, you do not want to waste money on ads that do not work but sometimes other things interfere, like the headlines of the day.

Thousands of dollars can be spent on marketing. We find that most self-publishers are on a tight budget and are not interested in spending large amounts of money to launch their book. But, if you are a celebrity or well-known in your field, a top publicity agent may be just what you may be looking for!

- Website sitebuilders
- Established websites
- WordPress
- Search Engine Optimization (SEO)
- Email list and newsletters

BUILD A WEBSITE
Online Authors

WEBSITES CAN BE INCREDIBLY POWERFUL FOR SELF-PUBLISHERS. Perhaps you will use your website address to link to your Amazon author page, book, or in your social media posts. It takes work to be discovered online even when you have a website.

QUICK TIPS

- Establish a website even before you complete a book.
- Buy your own domain name.
- Your email should use your domain name.
- Use keywords and keyword phrases on your site that are also used on your Amazon author page and books.
- Use social media.
- I recommend what I use, and that is WordPress® (.org, not .com), Genesis Framework with a Genesis child theme, and Yoast SEO.
- When building a brand, establish the CMYK colors first and work backwards to RGB color for website.

Website sitebuilders

Should you use a website sitebuilder or drag and drop builder? That depends on where your traffic will come from. The short answer is if you are not dependent on your site to generate traffic, you can use a website sitebuilder.

Good SEO is critical for a site without traffic, and that does not automatically happen. A site built with a sitebuilder is only good if a significant amount of traffic is referred from another source. This might be from your Amazon listing.

Authors should have no expectations of generating organic traffic if using a sitebuilder. Organic traffic is not guaranteed. But maybe a simple sitebuilder page on your own domain name is all you need.

Photo by Fikret Tozak on Unsplash

- Sitebuilders are cheap plus their basic site designs are often attractive. However, when content is added, the site might not look as you imagined.
- Sitebuilders are not the best choice for Search Engine Optimization. You have complete control over SEO with WordPress as you can edit the code as deep as you want to or as skills your allow. You cannot do this with sitebuilders. I do not code. I reccommend theYoast SEO plugin.
- Some sitebuilders are Adobe ® Flash Player ® based. Search engines cannot read Flash.
- Sitebuilders may offer only one-page sites.
- You are on a sitebuilder server with many other sites. It slows your site.
- Ads for the sitebuilder may appear on your site, depending on your plan.
- It is better to use your own domain. If you are using a sitebuilder URL address and later move to your own domain, all links will be lost. Maybe SEO will not matter with a sitebuilder URL, but it will matter when you move your site.
- Use an email address with your own domain name, book title, author name, or business. Do not use a web address with the name of the sitebuilder. You are viewed as more professional with an email address using your own domain. Anyone can use a generic like "gmail.com."

Examples: DOMAIN: AuthorBookStudio.com
EMAIL: BookTitle@AuthorBookStudio.com

Established websites

A website—especially an online store—must have high traffic to succeed and attract visitors who buy books or any other products or services offered. The best situation is to have an established website with followers. Book sales will happen, but you have earned it because you have likely been building your site and your following for some time.

It is especially important to start a website before you write a book. The goal is to build traffic and an email list. Existing websites already have content that many people search for if they have a niche and good SEO. The site may work well organically with somewhat unique keywords that are not too obscure.

Let us assume that you self-published a cookbook. There are many cookbooks for sale in the marketplace, so you have competition. Drill down as far as you can, writing posts with keywords and longtail keywords. Search competitors' sites for the keywords that they are using.

An existing website does not guarantee the needed traffic to sell books. Even if you have a great website and solid SEO, you may still need to spend money on advertising.

Be sure to send existing or prospective customers an email to sign up. They may be extremely interested in news about your book launch. Send them emails about any other books you publish, or products and services that you may offer now or in the future.

CONNECT WITH VISITORS

A website can instead be a place where buyers come to learn more about your product or service. They need to be directed to the site especially when a search engine does not bring the desired results.

However you use your website, it is very important to connect with the people who may be interested in your book(s) if you are an author or self-publisher. It is equally important if you are a small publisher. Keep in touch with your email list to announce the book launch, a new book review, or insights on something that you write about or photograph. Promote a new post or page. Offer information, A second printing is news, especially if you have just penned a new title. Do you have any other products on your website to promote?

BOOK RETAIL PRICING

Charge the full retail price for your book on your website. However, realize that while you have buyers who come to your website, most of them just want more information. Friends may buy at the retail price on your site. But the average buyer will head over to Amazon to find a lower price.

We advise self-publishers to print their books with our company because Star Print Brokers prints and binds the best books anywhere.

Sell your books on Amazon because they have more traffic than any other website. Get exposure to the largest audience of book buyers. Use their "Look Inside" add on.

Target other places for potential book sales, like groups you belong to, Barnes & Noble, or brick and mortar bookstores.

WordPress

There are many paths to follow when creating a website. It would be overwhelming to discuss all the possibilities here, but we can give you an overview and provide information about what we have learned in more than 20 years of building and maintaining our websites.

I built the Star Print Brokers website in November 1998 with an early sitebuilder. I made the switch from that sitebuilder to WordPress in 2010. We continue to use WordPress today.

There have been many changes since then. I am a fan of WordPress, owning your own domain, using Genesis as a framework, and a good child theme that works with Genesis. Whenever I built a site using WordPress but not Genesis, I ran into security concerns, or the theme would just break. That is just my experience. Your experience may be different.

If I were to do something different, I would buy one of the top-selling WordPress themes from ThemeForest, since there have been so many sales over many years. Also, many people swear by Divi, made by Elegant Themes. But, I can only recommend what has worked for us.

WORDPRESS.COM VERSUS WORDPRESS.ORG

WordPress.*com* is okay for small blogs, but we do not recommend it for a business website.

WordPress.*org* is where you can get WordPress and plugins. WordPress is a CMS (Content Management System) used by thirty percent of all websites at this writing.

Road Map to building a WordPress website

HOSTING

Most hosting companies break down their WordPress website hosting options into several different plans, but do use a host that uses WordPress.

If you want a simple 1- to 3-page site, start with shared hosting. You can always upgrade. We use a managed hosting business plan with **SiteGround**. A number of years ago we switched from another host and have no complaints. The customer service is very good. Three other popular hosts for WordPress websites are WP Engine, Bluehost and DreamHost.

If a hosting company seems obscure or does not rank highly when you do a search, it may be that an entrepreneur is reselling a major host's services. That might be good if the host provides other services that you find helpful. Start by investigating the top hosting companies.

Incidentally, you can always migrate a WordPress website to another host. Sometimes there is a fee. There are plugins to migrate websites, so try doing it yourself. See https://WordPress.org/plugins. Always keep your site backed up. General hosting offerings:

Shared self-hosted: Inexpensive. Great for blogs and small websites.
Managed hosting: The cost might be higher but needed for bigger sites.
Cloud hosted: From $80 to $250 or more, for high-performing sites.

WORDPRESS

WordPress can be installed from your hosting panel, after you sign up for hosting. Make sure an SSL certificate is enabled. Select it as an option or contact support. Do not use "admin" for a user name. Use strong user names and passwords.

Whatever theme you choose, the installation of your child theme and required plugins will be covered in your host's set-up instructions. In fact, all set-ups to get your site running should be covered.

DOMAIN NAMES

There are places where you can get a domain name for free. To see availability of domain names go to a site like GoDaddy.com to see availability. The extension should be *.com*. Avoid hyphenated domain names or other extensions. Try to avoid domain names that are too long. A business site should have it's own domain. Frankly, we named our company in 1999, but now I would rather have something shorter that StarPrintBrokers.com.

I tried to check domain availability at SiteGround's domain names link. Instead of getting results, they wanted me to select a "New Hosting Plan." The $6.99 Start Up plan will be fine for building a site. You can then select the domain to buy at SiteGround or transfer a domain name. Check availability at another site like GoDaddy. Then buy the domain as your WordPress host.

GENESIS FRAMEWORK

When I switched to WordPress in 2010, I still found problems with the website theme. I tried different themes which always seemed to break the site. Just last year, I tried a WordPress theme that was not compatible with Genesis Framework. The Genesis Framework provides a solid foundation and is search engine optimized. Use Genesis-friendly child themes.

You can buy Genesis Framework at StudioPress.com currently sold for $59.95. Alternatively, buy a Child Theme and Genesis for around $129.95.

Studio Press was bought by WP Engine, where you can also host your site. You get free access and support for StudioPress themes and Genesis Framework if you sign up for their hosting plan. If I ever leave SiteGround, WP Engine is a good option. As of this writing, SiteGround is no longer offering WordPress support. However, their help desk is very good, so we will stay with what is working.

CHILD THEMES

I suggest specifically looking for child themes that are for Genesis Framework. You can find them at StudioPress. I bought their Pro Package which means I have access to all their themes.

I tried out many child themes. Some were built by StudioPress and some are third-party builds. The theme we currently use on StarPrintBrokers.com is "Refined Pro," by Restored316. A lot depends on the instructions for the set-up of a child theme, and customer service. Restored 316 is professional and their instructions are easy to follow. Their support is wonderful. Restored316 has a Facebook community page where you may find many answers to theme questions. When considering a new theme for AuthorBookStudio.com, instead of using a child theme to which I have free access, I bought Restored 316's "Splendor Theme."

The StudioPress child themes take you through set-up of menus, comments, site title, tag line or logo image, reading settings, and widgets. They will also advise about needed plugins.

There are several child themes I encourage authors to use for selling books. Almost all the themes can be modified for use by self-publishers or small publishers. Instructions to set up your child theme will guide you through installation. However, any child theme can be modified.

- Author Pro Theme Package by StudioPress
- Navigation Pro by StudioPress
- Authority Pro Theme Package by StudioPress

WORDPRESS PLUGINS FOR AUTHORS

There are specific WordPress plugins for authors and publishers.

- Required plugins are suggested in set-up instructions for your chosen child theme.

- A plugin that is compatible with any Genesis Child Theme is Genesis Author Pro. It is free at WordPress.org. It creates a library which allows you to add books to your site.
- If you opt for a WordPress site and are selling one book, you need to use one of the following plugins available on WordPress.org/plugins:
  - WooCommerce to sell digital and physical books
  - Easy Digital Downloads for selling digital books

COLOR

When building a brand, establish the CMYK process color or PMS ink colors first. Work backwards to RGB for the website. That is because CMYK has a more limited color array than RGB. If you establish CMYK, it is easier to match them to RGB equivalents. See Chapter 2, *Planning a Book,* page 43.

I choose process color Pantone inks first from the Pantone Color Bridge Coated guide, and then use the RGB equivalent. HTML, CMYK, Spot, as well as RGB are on the guide as well.

Search Engine Optimization (SEO)

This is the means used to help pages rank higher in search engines such as Google. Search is one of the ways people find content online. The higher you rank with search engines, the better the chance to increase traffic on your website.

When someone searches for you, your book or company by name, like "BettyJoDiet.com", you will likely be found online. But, if you are unknown to them and they search for a common keyword phrase like: "diet cookbook", "book", "author", "recipes"—you might show up a thousand pages behind the first page search results. Starting out, you have no real page ranking.

How can you be found? People need to be directed to your site and higher ranking websites take time to develop. Results may be time-consuming or expensive to achieve on a new site. Getting traffic is the hard part. But, even if your site has very little traffic, it is important to have an online presence.

Potential buyers may be coming from a link on your Amazon Author page or your book listing on Amazon. They are looking for more information. They may be wondering if they want to buy your French cookbook for example, or another French cookbook that they see on Amazon. Shoppers often want more information to make a buying decision.

Maybe you have a French cookbook and are writing specifically about Parisian recipes paired with wines from the south of France. You might make suggestions for fine wines from different regions in the USA as well as France. Champagne with crêpes is delicious, as is crêpes and a sparkling wine from California!

Check the Google Keyword Tool to see how many searches there are for competitor's keywords or any keywords you would like to use in website pages or posts. A keyword may be "cookbook," but thousands of people search for cookbooks. You are not likely to find yourself on page one of Google searches. No one can guarantee that, so do not believe the SEO junk emails arriving in your inbox. A long-tailed keyword (phrase) may be "parisian cookbook," or "california sparkling wine."

Self-publishers need a beautiful, professional-looking website, and it should be as professional as your book. There is no guarantee of high website ranking results or book sales, but supplying information to buyers on your site is still a key factor for success.

I am a fan of WordPress and the Yoast SEO plugin. Yoast is currently the number one WordPress SEO plugin. I have been using it for many years. In my opinion, everyone needs to invest in the premium version.

Before you write any pages or posts, learn about how to write posts for best results. Research keyword phrases with Google Keyword tool. Better yet, find related keyword phrases inside the post editor of the latest Yoast SEO plugin. Keywords can be taken directly from your book. They may lay the foundation for being found on the web and for keyword usage on Amazon.

You will get many emails from those who want to help you with Search Engine Optimization (SEO) or website building. The first thing to check is their email domain. How serious can these people be if their email domain is: @gmail.com, @outlook.com, @yahoo.com, etc. Our email domain addresses are all @StarPrintBrokers.com. Even if a person represents a small company, they should have a business email address, as should an author, publisher, or designer. Why would you do business and spend money with someone with a generic email address? How can you take them seriously?

Good SEO services are not cheap. It takes about four months for better ranking results. Even with the best SEO in place on your site, you will still have to write posts with keywords.

Most authors just want a destination website for their potential buyers. They may use their site as a validation of their author page and book sales on Amazon. First, do your research for keywords to use on Amazon. Search for which categories your book will be listed. Whenever possible, use the same keywords on your site that you will be using on Amazon.

Email list and newsletters

Lay the foundation for book sales. An email list is a good way to stay in touch with readers who are interested in your writing, books, products, or services. Stay in touch with recent book buyers.

Getting traffic

Do you need traffic? It is a serious question and most often the answer is: Yes! You need traffic to build an email list. If you are going to be in contact with readers and book buyers on a regular basis, having lots of traffic is a must fo securing legitimate email subscribers. This is particularly important if you have an online store.

SELLING ON YOUR WEBSITE

If you choose to make your site the destination, then you need to be writing many pages and posts. Optimize those by including images on your site and in your store.

Due to the nature of our business, Star Print Brokers puts in a great deal of time and effort into building and maintaining our website. Our business is brokering the printing of high-quality books. We also offer book design services. We do not need Amazon for marketing the services that we offer.

When I started to write *Book Design: Simple & Professional*, I needed another website to promote the book, linking to Amazon for book sales. There are plans for several more books in the *Simple & Professional* series. AuthorBookStudio.com was created without expectation of immediate high-traffic. We are creating posts and pages for the site and optimizing keywords. Some visitors will find us this way. But more book buyers will find us on Amazon with searches that describe the books we sell or specific subject matter.

Perhaps you have already experimented with various keywords on your website. The same website keywords may be helpful on Amazon. If you wrote a cookbook for your restaurant, the more pertinent keywords might be more specific, like "seafood cookbook," or more specifically "salmon seafood cookbook." How about "blackened salmon seafood cookbook"?

Use longtail keyword phrases as well as single keywords. While there are a number of sites that offer keyword research tools, you can check results with the Google Keyword Planner at https://ads.google.com/home/tools/keyword-planner/.

While you can start with the Yoast SEO free plugin, I found the Premium version to be invaluable. The free version is fine for a site with limited content. Depending on your products, services, and website, try their Local SEO, Video SEO, News SEO, and Yoast WooCommerce plugins.

AUTHOR PAGE ON AMAZON

Since being found on the web and building significant traffic is one of the hardest things to do—especially for a new self-publisher—then maybe just a website with links to Amazon is all you need initially. However, continue to collect names for important emails that must go out, like a new book launch.

Traffic is the biggest challenge and that is why I always recommend that self-publishers print with Star Print Brokers because we print the best books, Then sell your books on Amazon because they have an enormous amount of traffic which your website cannot match.

As of this writing, the top websites with the most traffic on the planet are in this order: Google, YouTube, Facebook, and Amazon. How are book buyers going to find you? If they are not already aware of your specific book or your name, they will go to Amazon to buy a book. Even if they know you or your book and do a search on Google, they may very well find you on Amazon as well as your website.

Sign up for an author page on Amazon. List all book titles for sale. You can either fulfill orders yourself, or have Amazon fulfill the orders at an additional cost. I suggest that if you are a new self-publisher and have 1,000 books or less, fulfill the orders yourself. If you print more than that, have us send them to Amazon for fulfillment. You will need to find out from Amazon which warehouse they will be delivered to. We need this information for the quote, as the destination and any split shipping changes the quote.

Use Amazon's "Look Inside" feature. While it is a small additional cost, book buyers like to see a sample of what they are getting before they buy. It may well increase the number of sales for your book.

The most important thing you can do to be found is to be listed in appropriate Amazon categories and use unique keywords that people may be searching for. A keyword can be one word or a phrase.

WEBSITE SIGNUP FORMS

Typically, people find your website and then use a form to sign up to receive your newsletter or email updates. Always put the newsletter or email sign up form on the home page. Visitors are more likely to sign up if they are offered a freebie of some sort. They are called lead magnets. Here are some ideas of things that you might offer:

- A free ebook or guide.
- A discount on a product or service.
- Percentage or dollar amount discount off first order.
- Promote your "subscriber only" benefits.
- Download a free article or how-to.
- Download a chapter or part in a book.
- A PDF with a sampling of something you sell.
- Download a free checklist or a list of something particular to your business,
- Offer a free mini-course.
- A free Cheat Sheet or Hack.

Email marketing software

MailChimp is fairly easy to use and free to start with. We are using it currently. Most of the email services are free until you reach a certain number of subscribers.

Some of the other services are ActiveCampaign, Constant Contact, Convert Kit, Drip (for ecommerce), Emma, HubSpot, iContact, MailerLite, MailPoet, Moosend, Pardot by Salesforce, SendInBlue, and more. I am not endorsing any of these services. Email marketing software may have different uses, complexities, costs, and functions. Know who your prospective client is, and do not turn them off!

Have you ever been interested in taking an online course? You probably expect to receive a number of emails that are sent on a pre-determined schedule. That is usually fine with most people, as they want the course and information. However, if they are no longer interested in a product or service, but are emailed daily or even every other day, they unsubscribe and sometimes block the offending email address. The point is that there is a distinct difference between providing valuable information and pestering people. Know your audience!

Glossary
Resources
Fractional equivalents: pounds / points / GSM
Paper equivalents in Asia & Europe vs. USA
Comparable Pounds to GSM paper weight
Chart for other paper needs
Index

GLOSSARY

AA　An abbreviation for *author's alteration*. Changes or corrections requested by author after art has been submitted. An AA is charged an additional cost based on an hourly rate.

acid-free paper　Stock having a pH of, or close to 7. The deterioration of acid-free paper happens at a slower rate, giving the paper a longevity.

adhesive binding　Glued binding instead of stitched binding to hold pages or signatures in place. Adhesive bindings are perfect binding, notch binding, and burst binding.

against the grain　Folding or printing on press at a right angle to the grain direction of the paper.

alignment　The position of text in the margins. Justified text is flush with the margins on both sides. Text can be aligned on one margin, either the left or right, called left-justified or right-justified, ragged-left or ragged-right, or flush-left or flush-right.

aqueous coating　Water based coating applied by printing press over printing.

Arabic numerals　Many type fonts make two forms available: *lining* or *aligning* (1 2 3 4 5 6 7 8 9 0), and *old style* (1 2 3 4 5 6 7 8 9 0). See **Roman numerals**.

artwork　Images, including photos, maps, drawings, incorporated into the book design for reproduction.

ascender　The part of a lowercase letter that ascends above the x-height, in letters like b, d, f, h, k, l. See **descender**.

baseline　Capital and lowercase letters sit on the baseline. The three parts of letters are the ascenders, descenders, and x-height.

back matter　All content that follows the body or text matter.

banding　A striation or a streak gradient within a solid area. It is undesirable, but sometimes shows up in digitally output proofs or books. Striations will not print in books printed on press, but can appear when books are digitally output.

barcode　An EAN Bookland barcode is specifically for printed books. It contains the ISBN and retail price of the book. A barcode may be reduced in size to 80 percent, but 92 percent is standard. The barcode is placed on the lower right corner of the back cover but not too close to the spine.

baseline　The imaginary line on which most of the characters in a typeface sit.

binding　The covering of a book such as leather, cloth, coated papers. Also, to compile leaves or signatures together with glue, stitching, sewing or other means to keep together.

binding cloth　A fabric that has been treated to affix to books as cover wrapping. It comes is different weights, colors, textures, and patterns.

bindery　Department within a printing plant that folds, cuts, collate, drills, binds printed pieces or books. At times, some or all bindery services are contracted though an outside bindery.

bitmap　A black and white art file format that is, lacking any gray tones.

bleed　To run an image over the edge of a sheet or page and then trim after printing. A bleed is usually 3 mm, or 1/8 inch (0.125 inch).

blind folio　The page number is not printed on the page. This could be a blank page.

Photo by Alif Caesar Rizqi Pratama on Unsplash

blind stamp   A blind stamp may be used on a book cover and / or on the spine. A die is made for provided text, usually the title and author's name. The text die is pressed or stamped into the cover. No foil is applied. See **foil stamping** and **stamping**.

blueline   A type of proof. The page(s) and / or plate(s) to be printed show up in blue. A blueline is a position proof, as are the Ozalid, blueprint, diazo, Dylux, Vandyke, and a brownline, among others. It is proof of film, and not a proof of the process color. These kinds of proofs are not meant to be proofread for content.

board paper   Board is paper at or over 110-pound index, 80-pound cover, or 200 gsm. This type of board is used for soft cover book covers.

boards   Refers to the greyboard that is the stiffening material for a hard case book. That is a hardcover book.

body copy   Formatted type used for text, versus type used for heading, subheads, titles, chapter headings, etc.

book block   Books printed on press are printed in signatures. The signatures are folded and gathered to form a book block which are sewn or glued together.

bottom margin   The margin at the bottom of the page.

burst binding   The book spine is perforated and glued. Also see **Perfect binding** and **Notch binding.**

C1S and C2S   Abbreviations for "coated one side" and "coated two sides" referring to this type of paper.

caption   Text displayed next to an image describing a photo, chart, or illustration.

case bound   Encasing a book in a hard case made of gray board covered with leather, vinyl coated material, cloth, or paper.

character   In typography, a letter, numeral, or punctuation mark. Other special elements in a font are called *glyphs*. Variations of letters contained in the font may also be termed glyphs.

character style   Features are assigned to a typeface for a specific typographic use.

CMYK   Abbreviation for Cyan, Magenta, Yellow, and blacK, the four process colors used in the printing process. See **RGB**.

coated paper   A clay coating is applied to coated paper. In Asia, it is commonly provided in gloss and matte finishes. See **uncoated paper** and **woodfree paper.**

color correct   To change or adjust process colors. Generally, it is done correctly by professionals under controlled lighting such as a color booth.

Color Key   The brand name for color proof that overlays each plate to form the composed color.

color separation   (1) Breaking down continuous tone color images into four screened process inks suitable for printing on press. Can be scanned on a drum or flatbed scanner, and digitally separated. (2) The final color separated for four-color process printing.

color transparency   Transparent film used to make color separations. A 35 mm slide is an example of a color transparency.

concealed Wire-O binding   A binding using a continuous double wire, threaded through punched holes. The concealed binding has a spine. It can be hardcover or soft cover. See **concealed Wire-O binding** and **Wire-O binding.**

continuous tone   Describes images such as photographs and illustrations that have not been prepared for printing. They do not have a dot pattern. A photo print taken with a camera and developed in a dark room on photo paper, has a continuous tone.

copyfitting   Adjusting the size and spacing of type to make it fit within an area.

cover   The front, back and spine of a book are considered the cover. They should be set-up in a new InDesign document to print on one page. If the inside covers are to be printed, create a side 2.

cover wrap   The covering material used on the greyboard of a hard case book. It may be cloth, paper, vinyl, bonded leather, or leather. Often the paper is printed with a design like the dust jacket.

crop marks   Lines indicating trim and bleed.

cyan   One of the four process colors including Cyan, Magenta, Yellow and blacK, (CMYK).

deboss   To press an image so that it lies below the surface. It is the opposite of emboss – to raise the image above the surface.

deckle edge   A deckle edge is the untrimmed edges of the paper. It is a feathery edge formed when the pulp flows against the deckle. The deckle is also the wet sheet off the wire of a paper manufacturing machine.

descender The part of a lowercase letter that descends below the baseline in letters like g, j, p, y. See **ascender**.

die Custom made from metal according to the designer's file. A die is used to cut, score, stamp, emboss, and deboss.

die cut To cut shapes or special edges on paper using a die. It is custom manufactured.

digital press Equipment like a high-end photocopier, used to print books, a page or two at a time, with toner instead of ink on a commercial printing press. Also see **web press**, **offset press**, and **sheet-fed press.**

digital proofing Proofs produced from digital files lasered or ink jetted on paper.

dingbats Character glyphs consisting of graphic symbols such as bullets, dividers, and other graphic ornaments.

discretionary hyphen A hyphen that is invisible unless needed to break a word. See **soft hyphen.**

display type This is type that is larger than body text. Display type is used for headlines and special use display.

dots per inch (dpi) The number of dots in a one-inch line. It refers to the resolution of the printer. See **pixels per inch.**

double bump To print a single image twice so it has two layers of ink. Set it up in InDesign. Discuss the set-up first with the printer.

drill To drill a hole in the text block or printed matter. Printers machine drill the holes.

drop cap The first capital letter of a paragraph is set in a larger point size. It lines up with the base of a second, third, or lowest line of the paragraph. A drop cap may be used to indicate the start of a new section, such as a chapter. See **initial cap** (raised cap).

dummy An example of what the final product may look like. Usually made up of plain stock. Sometimes the cover wrap used is what was quoted to the client. Also called a mock-up.

duotone Duotones are grayscale images printed with two inks.

dust jacket A loose paper wrapping for a hard case or perfect bound book. Also called a jacket, it has inside front cover and inside back cover flaps. The dust jacket and flaps often contain promotional information. Also see **French fold dust jacket.**

ellipsis A punctuation character made up of three periods in a row. The character can be used, but it is better to type set thin en spaces between periods. It replaces a word or phrase that has been left out. E*xample*: **this …**

em, em space, em quad An em is the width of the point size. *Example:* in 10-point type, one em has a width of 10 points.

em dash An em dash is used to indicate—a break—as just used twice in this sentence. If the em dash touches adjacent characters, a thin space may be added on either side of the em dash.

emboss To press an image into paper so that it sits above the surface as a raised image or type. Embossing is a common option added to book titles on the cover or dust jacket of a book.

en, en space, en quad An en is half the width of the point size, or half the width of an em space.

en dash An en dash is used to indicate a range, such as 2000–2020. If the en dash touches adjacent characters, add a thin space on either side of an en dash.

endnotes Numbered notes collected at the end of a book or chapter that replaces footnotes.

endpapers Folded sheets that are glued to the inside front and back cover of a case bound (hardcover) book. Endpapers can be plain white, printed, or a specialty paper that comes in different colors and finishes. Soft cover books do not have endpapers. Additionally, endpapers are also called endsheets.

epigraph A quotation in the front matter of a book.

EPS Encapsulated Postscript format is a graphics file format used in vector or bitmap graphics used in Adobe Illustrator and Photoshop.

exact match color A term to describe matching original samples like a fabric swatch, continuous tone photo, print, or supplied proof. See **pleasing color.**

fifth color Ink color used in addition to the four CMYK inks needed for four-color process printing. It is a spot ink.

film laminate A permanent covering used to protect the cover of a printed book cover. It can be matte or gloss.

finished size The size of printed item after trimming or folding. Also called trim size. The flat size would be a different measurement.

flat size   The size of a printed item after trimming but before folding.

flood varnish   A matte or gloss varnish that covers the entire page or pages. No additional Indesign file or PDF needs to be created. See **spot color, spot varnish or spot UV.**

flush-left / ragged-right   Text aligned on the left margin is flush-left. Text unaligned on the right margin, so it has a ragged edge, is called flush-left / ragged-right. Also, another term is simply ragged-right.

foil emboss   To foil emboss is to apply a foil stamp to a raised type or image. Foil emboss is commonly applied to a dust jacket.

foil stamp   A foil stamp may be used on a book cover and / or the spine. A die is made for a provided image, usually the title and author's name. The image is pressed or stamped into the cover and foil is applied to the impression. See **blind stamp** and **stamping**.

folio   The page number in a book.

font   One style, weight, and width of a typeface. Four examples are: Garamond Regular, Italic, Bold, and Bold Italic.

footnote   Note that appears at the bottom of a page.

format   The style, shape, size and layout determined for a book design.

four-color process printing   Full color printing uses CMYK, or Cyan, Magenta, Yellow, and blacK inks. The shorthand for 4-color process on both sides on a page is 4 / 4 or 4C / 4C. Four-color process printing on one side is 4 / 0 or 4C / 0C.

French flaps   Extended front and / or back cover on a perfect bound book.

French fold dust jacket   A dust jacket that has a fold on the top and bottom provides for a more finished appearance and durability. Also see **dust jacket**.

front matter   All content preceding the body or text matter.

GBC binding   A plastic comb binding. Holes are punched into the pages. It's not suitable for professional book binding. See **mechanical binding.**

GIF   Graphics Interchange Format, for use on the Internet. Use TIFs and JPGs for printing. Pronounced "jiff" not "giff".

GSM   The unit of measurement for paper weight (grams per square meter).

galley proof   A proof of typeset text that has not yet been paginated.

gathered   Signatures assembled in the correct order for binding.

ghost halftone   A digital image whose density has been scaled back so that it is a faint or ghosted image.

gilding   To gild the edges of a book with gold leaf. Bibles and special edition books may have gilding.

grammage   Basis weight and grammage of paper in grams per square meter (gsm). It is the standard in Asia and Europe.

gray component replacement (GCR)   A process of replacing gray tones in the cyan, yellow, and magenta films. It is used to reduce the amount of ink.

gray scale   Strip of values. Black and white photos contain grey tones, so are greyscale.

gutter   The two inside margins that meet in the center of the book.

halftone   *Verb:* To scan a continuous tone image and convert it to a halftone by means of adding a dot pattern. *Noun:* A screened image is called a halftone.

hanging indent   The first line in front of the rest of the text. Quotes, when stylized and not part of a paragraph, are set with an open quote mark in front of the text, the hanging indent.

hardcover   Case bound books are called hardcover books or hard bound. They are bound with stiff board called greyboard. The covering material is the cover wrap. It is glued to the greyboard. Cover wrap can be paper, cloth, linen, leather, suede, vinyl, faux cloth, faux linen, faux leather, and more.Some case bound books use a thin, flexible board rather than a thick board.

head bands and tail bands   The decorative cloth on the top and bottom of the spine of a professionally bound hardcover book.

head margin   The margin at the top of the page.

heading   The title of a text section or part.

hyphen   A short dash used in a phone number or between words. A hyphen is shorter than an en dash or an em dash.

ICC color profile   Ask your printer for the ICC profile to use for their output. ICC was established by the International Color Consortium.

ISBN   International Standard Book Number, a number assigned to a published work. It is on the copyright page. To get an ISBN, go to ISBN.org.

imposition   The correct arrangement of pages in a book signature after it is folded. This is handled by the printer.

impression   An impression is one sheet passing through a unit of a press.

initial cap   The first capital letter of a paragraph is set in a larger point size. It lines up with the base of the first line of text. It is also called *raised cap*. See **drop cap.**

ink jet printing   Method of printing by spraying droplets of ink. This is not used for books printed on a printing press. Also called jet printing.

inside margin   The gutter margin, where facing pages meet.

JPEG (.jpg)   Joint Photographic Experts Group. A file format used in digital cameras, on the web, and in book design and production. TIFF images are also used in book design.

K   One of the four process colors including Cyan, Magenta, Yellow, and blacK, (CMYK).

kerning   Adding or narrowing the space between two characters. It is different than tracking. See **tracking.**

ladder   A ladder is a series of consecutive lines, each ending with a hyphen. They look like the rungs of a ladder.

laminate   A clear sheet applied to hardcover and soft cover books with printed cover wrap. It protects the surface and comes in gloss and matte finishes.

landscape   The landscape-orientation means it is horizontal. The width of a book is greater than the height. The opposite is portrait-orientation that is vertical.

lay flat binding   A kind of binding that allows a publication to lie fully open, with a hollow back.

leading   Amount of space between lines of type. Goes back to the days of hot type, where lead (metal) lines were places between sections of type. See **linespacing.**

leaf   One sheet of paper in a book. Each side of a leaf is one page. Each leaf equals two pages.

letterspacing   The space between letters in the same word. See **kerning** and **tracking.**

ligature   Two letters as one character. *Examples:* ff, fi, ffl, Th.

line art   Images that are black and white. They can be bitmap or black ink.

linespacing   Amount of space between lines of type. Goes back to the days of hot type, where lead (metal) lines were places between sections of type. Also see **leading.**

lining figures   Arabic numerals that are the same as the uppercase letters in a font. See **oldstyle figures.**

lightweight paper   Book paper with basis weight less than 40#, 40 pound, which is equivilent to 60 gsm, grams per square meter.

loupe   A magnifying lens that stands upright on a surface. It is used to inspect proofs, color, printing, etc. It is also called a glass. Another similar item is a linen tester.

magenta   One of the four process colors including Cyan, Magenta, Yellow, and blacK, (CMYK).

makeready   The set-up and detail work to ensure proper printing and binding for a book. It is the printing and bindery set-up.

manuscript   An author's original work in any form such as digital, typed, handwritten, a printout.

margin   The white space around the edge of the page.

matte finish   Low sheen flat (not gloss) finish on coated paper.

mechanical binding   A term that describes binding materials using a plastic comb, plastic or metal spiral coil, 3-ring binder, or a technique not requiring gluing, sewing, or stitching. See **GBC.**

mil 1/1000 Inch   The thickness of plastic films, "mils." The measurement for plastic sleeves for CDs or DVDs are expressed in mils.

mockup   An example of what the final book may look like. Usually made of white stock and may or may not be the quoted stock. Also called a dummy.

notch binding   Spine notched and glued. Also see **Perfect binding** and **Burst binding.**

oldstyle figures   Arabic numerals that are the same size as the lowercase letters in a font. See **lining figures** and **tabular figures.**

offset press   Most commonly used for 1,000 books or more. Ink is offset from plate to blanket, then blanket the impression on paper. High-quality books are printed on offset, sheet-fed presses. See **digital press**, **web press**, and **sheet-fed press.**

Open Type A cross-platform font format for both Windows and Macintosh. Open Type contains many features such as buildable fractions, ligatures, oldstyle numerals, small caps, and some have extra glyphs and ornaments.

orphan A word, or part of a word appearing alone at the end of a paragraph at the *top* of a column or page. Avoid orphans by rewording or changing spacing. See **widow.**

over run Books printed in addition to the original quantity requested. Typically, the USA standard is plus or minus ten percent unless a request to print for "exact quantity" is received. In Asia, the range is two to five percent. Most of the time in Asia, the exact quantity is printed. 'Unders' refers to fewer copies than requested by the client. Also called 'overs and unders' on the printing contract.

page Each side of a leaf in a book is termed a page. One leaf equals two pages.

pagination The flow of pages in proper order throughout the book.

paragraph style Features are assigned to a paragraph style. They may include typeface, leading, color, tracking, rules, bullets, etc.

PDF (.pdf) Portable Document Format. An Adobe or other band name PDF that allows viewing and if given permission, may be edited. Adobe Acrobat is prefered.

perfect binding The spine of a book is roughened and glued before a soft cover is applied. Also see **Notch binding** and **Burst binding.**

pica A unit of measure approximately equal to 0.166 in. There are 12 points to a pica and 6 picas to an inch.

pixel A unit of a digital image. It is a scanner, computer, or other digitally generated dot.

pixels per inch (ppi) PPI describes the resolution of a digital image, not a physical, continuous-tone image. See **dots per inch.**

plate A printing plate contains the image to be reproduced on press.

pleasing color A term to describe average color. It may not match original samples such as a fabric swatch, a continuous tone photo, print, or supplied proof. See **exact match color.**

PMS Pantone Matching System.

PNG (.png) Portable Network Graphics. A file format that is used on the Internet. It should not be used for book printing.

point (pt) A unit of measure in typography equaling 1/12 pica or .013875 inch (.351 mm). There are 12 points to a pica and 6 picas to an inch.

portrait The portrait-orientation means vertical. The length of a book is greater than the width. The opposite is landscape, or horizontal.

prepress Procedures performed by the printer or service bureau to make art files ready to print. Prepress is also a department in a printing facility.

prepress proof A color proof, also called *dry proof*, and is made by a digital output device. It is not the same as a 'press proof' that is printed on a commercial printing press, with ink on paper instead of toner. A press proof is also not created with an inkjet printing device.

press check Press sheets that are examined before allowing printing to begin. Also an in-person press check.

press proof Proofs made on a commercial printing press before the job is started. The entire press must be set up, so press proofs are more costly than prepress proofs. See **wet proof.**

print-on-demand (POD) A method to 'print' a few books at a time. A file is output a page or two at a time on a digital output device. The pages are bound with glue for a soft cover binding. A hardcover is side-sewn which is not a method used with quality book printing on press.

process color The colors used for four-color process printing are Cyan, Magenta, Yellow, and blacK, (CMYK).

RGB The RGB mode is used on the web, where color is made from red, green, and blue. Digital cameras also produce images in RGB. Images should be converted to CMYK for book printing. See **CMYK.**

rag paper Stock or paper with a high content of cotton. It is currently not available for most commercial book printing except for major publishers printing in high volume for particular books expected to be best sellers.

recto A right-hand page.

recycled paper A stock made from paper that has been recycled.

register marks Short lines marking edges of paper, trim, or bleeds.

resolution Sharpness of an image. Books are printed at 300 pixels per inch. Higher resolution files may be processed, but the printed results will be 300 ppi.

rezing up Increasing resolution artificially in Photoshop. It is not advised as images may print looking pixilated although they may look fine on the monitor.

reverse Image or type produced reversing the ink color. White type on a black background is a reverse.

rich black 100 percent black plus another ink. While K=100 and C=60 is a common combination, check the PMS process color swatches for other possibilities.

Roman numerals Used in front matter page numbering, either in UPPERCASE (I, II, III, IV, V, VI, VII, VIII, IX , X), or lowercase (i, ii, iii, iv, v, vi, vii, viii, ix, x). See **Arabic numerals**.

running headers and footers There is a variety of ways to set up the page numbers, chapters, book title, perhaps the author's name, or sections. Information belongs on the top or bottom margins. It is a way for the reader to navigate the book.

saddle stitch A type of binding which staples folded sheets along the fold. This is inferior for book binding and does not allow for a spine. Most bookstores will not accept a book without a spine.

sans-serif font A typeface without serifs which are the small "feet" found on the characters. *Example:* Helvetica.

scanner Device used to scan an image. There are different types of scanners including a wide range of flatbed and drum scanners. Scan at 300 ppi *and* at the size to print or larger.

screen tint Color created by dot pattern rather than solid ink.

semi-concealed Wire-O binding Using a continuous double wire that is threaded through punched holes of the book. A semi-concealed binding can have wire visible on the spine, or on the back cover, next to the spine. Used for hardcover or soft cover. See **concealed Wire-O binding** and **Wire-O binding.**

serif A typeface with serifs which have the small "feet" on the characters. *Example:* Garamond.

sheet-fed press A press that prints sheets of paper. High-quality books are sheet-fed. See **digital press**, **offset press**, and **web press.**

signature A large printed sheet with an even number of pages printed front and back is then folded three times and trimmed to form a signature, like a booklet. They are then bound into a book. Pages do not fall out as is common with single sheet outputs for print-on-demand books.

small caps Small capital letters that are the same size as the x-height of lowercase letters. Typically used for A.M. or P.M.

Smyth Sewn Signatures that are sewn together before being bound as a hardcover or a soft cover book. It is a must for high page count books.

soft cover An example of a soft cover book is a paperback. They are perfect bound books that can be Smyth Sewn, notch or burst bound, or saddle stitched.

soft hyphen A hyphen that is invisible unless needed to break a word. See **discretionary hyphen.**

specifications Complete details of a book or any project to be printed. Ink, paper, binding, quantity, delivery location, as well as any specifics are detailed. Abbreviated as "specs."

spine The side or binding edge of a book. It is the area between the front cover and back cover. It will vary in width depending on the type of binding, the number of pages in the book, and paper thickness.

spiral bind A binding using a continuous wire or plastic, threaded through punched holes.

spot color, spot varnish or spot UV One ink, UV or a varnish applied to a specific portion of a page or pages. See **flood varnish.**

spread Pages that are side by side. Pages 2 and 3 would be a reader spread. Note: Page 1 in a book is always the first page and it is a right-hand page.

stamping A stamp may be used on a book cover and/or the spine. A die is made from a client provided image, or the title and author's name. The image is pressed or stamped into the cover with a specially made die. Then, an optional foil is applied to the stamped. See **foil stamp**.

standard viewing conditions Color as viewed a color viewing booth under 5000 K Kelvin lamps.

tabular figures Evenly spaced numerals that align in columns. See **lining figures** and **oldstyle figures.**

text matter   All content between the front matter and back matter.

TIFF (.tif) Tagged Image File Format   A stable file format commonly used for images in graphic design.

tip-in   Usually a single page, tipped into a book at the front or between signatures.

tip-on   A tip-on image is printed, trimmed to size, and has a permanent adhesive backing . It is applied to the cover of a book, usually with a foil stamp title.

tracking   Adding or subtracting the amount of space between groups of letters or lines of type. It is different than kerning. See **kerning.**

transparency   A positive photographic image that allows light to come through. An example is a 35 mm slide.

trim size   The size of a printed item after it is printed and then trimmed to size.

typeface family   Similar fonts derived from the same typeface. The Helvetica family for example, includes several styles, widths, and weights.

uncoated paper   Simply, paper that has not been coated. See **coated paper** and **woodfree paper.**

UCR Under Color Removal   When making color separations a portion of the of cyan, magenta and yellow ink is removed and black ink is added.

UV Coating   A liquid coating applied to a printed sheet. It is cured to bond with UV light.

varnish   A thin coating applied over a printed sheet for protection and appearance.

verso   A left-hand page.

vector image   Images created in Adobe Illustrator are vector images. They can be printed in any size without losing quality.

viewing booth   A booth for proper viewing of prepress materials, especially color.

vignette   A graphic element or illustration that fades into the background paper.

web press   A press that prints using large rolls of paper versus a press that is sheet fed with sheets of paper. Hgh-quality books are printed on sheet-fed presses. Web presses are used for magazines, newspapers, direct mail, etc. See **digital press**, **offset press**, and **sheet-fed press.**

wet proof   A wet proof is an accurate proof as it is produced in the same way as the final book page. It is produced on the same stock used to print the book. See **press proof.**

widow   A short line or single word at the *end* of a paragraph. Avoid by editing text or modifying spacing to lengthen or lose the line. See **orphan.**

Wire-O binding   A binding using a continuous double wire, threaded through punched holes. The standard binding has no spine. It can be hardcover or soft cover. Also see **concealed Wire-O binding** plus the **semi-concealed Wire-O binding.**

wood free paper   Made with a chemical pulp only. Wood free paper is an uncoated paper stock, typically used for novels, paperback books, and standard for the endpapers in hardcover books. See **coated paper** and **uncoated paper.**

x-height   The measurement of letters from the baseline to the top of a lowercase letter having nc ascenders or descenders, like c, e, m, n, o, r, s, u, v, w, x, z.

yellow   One of the four process colors including Cyan, Magenta, Yellow, and blacK, (CMYK).

RESOURCES

The following are some of my favorite resources. They are listed in categories and in alphabetical order.

PHOTOS & IMAGES

Creative Market
DesignCuts
Getty Images
Upsplashed

TYPE

Adobe Fonts
Emigre Fonts
Font Squirrel
Google Fonts
Laura Worthington Design
Mark Simonson
MyFonts
Sharp Type
TypeTogether
Typewolf

WORDPRESS

Easy Digital Downloads
Genesis Framework
StudioPress
WordPress.org
WooCommerce
WP Beginner
Yoast

GENESIS CHILD THEMES

Restored316
StudioPress

WEB HOSTING

BlueHost
SiteGround
WP Engine

INDESIGN INSTRUCTION

Adobe InDesign Help
CreativePro
Lynda.com

BOOKS

Graphic Artists Guild Handbook,
    Pricing & Ethical Guidelines
        by Graphic Artists Guild
Grid Systems in Graphic Design
        by Joseph Müller-Brockmann
The Chicago Manual of Style
        by University of Chicago Press
The Elements of Typographic Style
        by Robert Bringhurst

FRACTIONAL EQUIVALENTS:
POUNDS / POINTS / GSM

There are times when working in InDesign that you need to find the equivalent of a fraction, decimal, or millimeter. This is a chart to copy and save. It may also be helpful to go to **Edit** > **References** > **Units & Increments** and select a different horizonal & vertical **Ruler Unit**.

FRACTION	DECIMAL	MM		FRACTION	DECIMAL	MM
$1/64$	.0156	0.396		$33/64$	.5156	13.096
$1/32$	.0312	0.793		$17/32$	.5312	13.493
$3/64$	.0468	1.190		$35/64$	.5468	13.890
$1/16$	**.0625**	**1.587**		**$9/16$**	**.5625**	**14.287**
$5/64$	.0781	1.984		$37/64$	.5781	14.684
$3/32$	.0937	2.381		$19/32$	.5937	15.081
$7/64$	.1093	2.778		$39/64$	.6093	15.478
$1/8$	**.125**	**3.175**		**$5/8$**	**.625**	**15.875**
$9/64$	.1406	3.571		$41/64$	.6406	16.271
$5/32$	.1562	4.968		$21/32$	.6562	16.668
$11/64$	.1718	4.365		$43/64$	.6718	17.065
$3/16$	**.1875**	**4.762**		**$11/16$**	**.6875**	**17.462**
$13/64$	.2031	5.159		$45/64$	.7031	17.859
$7/32$	.2187	5.556		$23/32$	.7187	18.256
$15/64$	.2343	5.953		$47/64$	.7343	8.653
$1/4$	**.250**	**6.350**		**$3/4$**	**.750**	**19.050**
$17/64$	.2656	6.746		$49/64$	.7656	19.446
$9/32$	.2812	7.143		$25/32$	.7812	19.843
$19/64$	.2968	7.540		$51/64$	.7968	20.240
$5/16$	**.3125**	**7.937**		**$13/16$**	**.8125**	**20.637**
$21/64$	.3281	8.334		$53/64$	.8281	21.034
$11/32$	.3437	8.731		$27/32$	.8437	21.431
$23/64$	.3593	9.128		$55/64$	.8593	21.828
$3/8$	**.375**	**9.525**		**$7/8$**	**.875**	**22.225**
$25/64$	.3906	9.921		$57/64$	.8906	22.621
$13/32$	.4062	10.318		$29/32$	.9062	23.018
$27/64$	.4218	10.715		$59/64$	.9218	23.415
$7/16$	**.4375**	**11.112**		**$15/16$**	**.9375**	**23.812**
$29/64$	.4531	11.509		$61/64$	.9531	24.209
$15/32$	.4687	11.906		$31/32$	.9687	24.606
$31/64$	.4543	12.303		$63/64$	.9843	25.003
$1/2$	**.500**	**12.700**		**1**	**1.000**	**25.400**

PAPER EQUIVALENTS: ASIA & EUROPE VS. USA

This chart compares the paper weights commonly used for book printing in Asia and Europe to USA paper weights. First, you have to know:

- Asia and Europe measure stock in **Grams Per Square Meter (GSM)**
- USA measures in **pounds** and **points**

The GSM listed is the weight of the paper used by Star Print Brokers when printing in Asia. The USA pound and point weights are a calculation, so the USA paper weight might not exist.

HOW PAPER WEIGHT IS MEASURED

Basis weight: Used in the USA. It is the weight in pounds ("lb" or "#"). *A ream is 500 sheets.* The paper can be different types and weights. The basis weight is based on a ream.

Metric system: Used in Asia and Europe. It uses grammage, the weight of *one square meter of paper stock.* Grammage is measured by Grams per Square Meter (GSM.)

TEXT STOCK VERSUS COVER STOCK

The coated stock (first chart below) is for text stock, not cover stock. For instance, business cards are most often printed on a paper weight of 80 lb *cover* stock.

The 80 lb *text* and 80 lb *cover* paper weight stocks are different thicknesses. If business cards, for example, were printed on 80 lb *text* stock, they would be much thinner than *cover* stock.

Text Coated Stock
GLOSS ART OR MATTE ART
54 lb text weight = 80 gsm
61 lb text weight = 90 gsm
68 lb text weight = 100 gsm
82 lb text weight = 120 gsm
101 lb text weight = 150 gsm
122 lb text weight = 180 gsm
135 lb text weight = 200 gsm

Text Uncoated Stock
WOODFREE
54 lb text weight = 80 gsm
68 lb text weight = 100 gsm
81 lb text weight = 120 gsm
95 lb text weight = 140 gsm
95 lb text weight = 140 gsm
122 lb text weight = 180 gsm

Cover Stock for Soft Cover Books
ART BOARD; C1S, C2S, GLOSS ART, MATTE ART, & WOODFREE
8 pt cover weight = 190 gsm (actual stock closest is 180 gsm)
9 pt cover weight = 210 gsm (actual stock closest is 200 gsm)
10 pt cover weight = 230 gsm (actual stock closest is 250 gsm)
12 pt cover weight = 260 gsm (actual stock closest is 250 gsm)
14 pt cover weight = 310 gsm (actual stock closest is 300 gsm)
16 pt cover weight = 350 gsm
18 pt cover weight = 400 gsm

BOARD THICKNESS FOR HARDCOVER BOOKS

Binding Board for Hardcover Books
GREYBOARD
60 pt = 16 oz. = 1.4 mm = 1,000 gsm
65 pt = 20 oz. = 1.8 mm = 1,100 gsm
70 pt = 24 oz. = 2.0 mm = 1,200 gsm
80 pt = 28 oz. = 2.25 mm = 1,400 gsm

88 pt = 32 oz. = 2.5 mm = 1,600 gsm
92 pt = 36 oz. = 2.8 mm = 1,700 gsm
98 pt = 40 oz. = 3.0 mm = 1,800 gsm
140 pt = 48 oz. = 3.4 mm = 2,200 gsm

COMPARABLE POUNDS TO GSM PAPER WEIGHT

60 lb is comparable to 90 gsm
70 lb is comparable to 100 gsm
80 lb is comparable to 120 gsm

100 lb is comparable to 150 gsm
120 lb is comparable to 180 gsm
135 lb is comparable to 200 gsm

Star Print Brokers specializes in printing coffee table books. Using 120 gsm book paper weight is okay to avoid "show through." However, when we print coffee table books, art books, or photography books, we use 150 gsm or 180 gsm.

While it is possible to bind 200 gsm paper stock, it is the maximum paper weight that can be bound in a professionally printed book.

Note: C1S and C2S simply mean Coated 1 Side or Coated 2 Sides.

CHART FOR OTHER PAPER NEEDS

EQUIVALENT WEIGHTS

A ream = 500 sheets. Basis weight in pounds (#) is **bold.** The grammage (gsm) is **bold and in color.**

3 EXAMPLES: 100# BOOK is ± 148 gsm | 60# COVER is ± 162 gsm | 24# BOND is ± 61# BOOK

Grade of Paper	BOOK 25 X 38	BOND 17 X 22	COVER 20 X 26	BRISTOL 22.5 X 28.5	INDEX 25.5 X 30.5	TAG 24 X 36	Grammage GSM
BOOK	**30**	12	16	20	25	27	44
	40	16	22	27	33	36	59
	45	18	25	30	37	41	67
	50	20	27	34	41	45	74
	60	24	33	40	49	55	89
	70	28	38	47	57	64	104
	80	31	44	54	65	73	118
	90	35	49	60	74	82	133
	100	39	55	67	82	91	148
	120	47	66	80	98	109	178
BOND	33	**13**	18	22	27	30	49
	41	**16**	22	27	33	37	64
	51	**20**	28	34	42	46	75
	61	**24**	33	41	50	56	90
	71	**28**	39	48	58	64	105
	81	**32**	45	55	67	74	120
	91	**36**	50	62	75	83	135
	102	**40**	56	69	83	93	158
COVER	91	36	**50**	62	75	82	135
	110	43	**60**	74	90	100	162
	119	47	**65**	80	97	108	176
	146	58	**80**	99	120	134	216
	164	65	**90**	111	135	149	243
	183	72	**100**	124	150	166	271
BRISTOL	100	39	54	**67**	81	91	148
	120	47	65	**80**	98	109	178
	148	58	81	**100**	121	135	219
	176	70	97	**120**	146	162	261
	207	82	114	**140**	170	189	306
	237	93	130	**160**	194	216	351
INDEX	110	43	60	74	**90**	100	163
	135	53	74	91	**113**	122	203
	170	67	93	115	**140**	156	252
	208	82	114	140	**170**	189	328
TAG	110	43	60	74	90	**100**	163
	137	54	75	93	113	**125**	203
	165	65	90	111	135	**150**	244
	192	76	105	130	158	**175**	284
	220	87	120	148	180	**200**	326
	275	109	151	186	225	**250**	407

INDEX

A

Actual PPI, 60–61
Actual resolution, 63
Adobe Fonts, 8
Adobe InDesign. See InDesign
Adorn Ornaments Regular, 12
Advertisement design, 76–77
Alignment, 6, 30–31
Amazon, 162–163, 164–165, 173, 180
Ambroise Std Light, 19
Apostrophes, 31
ASIN (Amazon Standard Identification Number), 104
Audience, 5
Authors
    Amazon pages, 164, 165, 180
    branding, 160
    corrections, 58
    cover info, 55, 56
    responsibilities, 64
    working with, 65

B

Back cover, 55–57
Back matter, 68, 70, 71
Background art, 108
Bagged books, 110
Balance, 6
Barcodes, 56–57, 104, 105, 110, 158–159
Baseline grids, 77–80
Baskerville Regular, 17, 18
Belly bands, 126–127
Big Picture style, 75, 76–77
Black ink, 45
Bleeds, 28, 50, 51, 153
Board books, 88, 99
Body matter, 68, 70, 71
Bold type, 15–16, 97
Book and page documents, 92–95, 100–101
Book binding, 139–141
Book branding, 159
Book cover
    barcodes, 104, 105
    board books, 88
    ISBN, 104–105
    paper stock finish and ink selection, 146
    planning, 54–57
    retail price, 105–106
    spine width and printers' templates, 106–110
Book designer responsibilities, 64–65
Book page layout, 6–7, 14, 50–53
Book pricing, 105–106, 161–162, 173
Book sizes, standard, 35–38

Book sleeves, 131
Book structure, 67–71
Bookstore distribution, 164–165
Brand books, 160
Branding considerations, 159–160
Bumper boxes, 121
Burst bound books, 150

C

Capitalization, 23
Captions, 58
Center alignment, 31
Center Justify, 31
Century Gothic Regular, 17, 18
Chapters, creating, 94–95
Character styles, 15, 97
Charcuterie Serif Bold, 11
Child themes, 176
CIF (cost insurance freight), 166
CMYK
    about, 13, 141–142
    book interior and cover, 146
    color scheme, 43, 44
    endpapers, 147
    images, existing, 62
    reference books, 89
    text, 45–46
Coated paper, 38, 146, 197
Coca-Cola brand, 143
Coffee table books, 45, 50–52, 83, 120, 198
Color
    design fundamentals, 4, 13
    fonts, 40
    photographs and images, 59–60
    printing on press, 141–147
    reference books, 89
    scheme, 43–44
    shifting, 62
    text, 45–47
    variations in, 144–147
    websites, 177
Concealed Wire-O, 112, 148, 150
Content highlights, 56
Contrast, 7, 40–41
Cookbooks, 33, 83–84
Cover. See Book cover
Cover wraps, 82, 87, 109–110, 139
Curly quotes, 22

D

DDP (delivered duty paid), 166
Delivery and shipping costs, 165–166
Design fundamentals, 3–31

DesignCuts.com, 51–52
Destination space, 61, 145
Dingbats, 12
Direct mailers, 164
Distribution, 164–166
Divisions, book, 67–71
Document grids, 77
Documents, book and page, 92–95, 100–101
Domain names, 175
Duotones, 118–119
Dust jackets, 57, 87, 109, 112–113, 125–126, 139

E

EAN Bookland barcodes, 56–57, 104, 105, 110, 158–159
Effective PPI, 60–61
Effective resolution, 63
Ellipses, 27
Em dashes, 26
Email marketing software, 181
Emphasis, 15–16, 29
En dashes, 26
Endpapers, 87, 115–117, 133, 139, 141, 146–147
Exact match color, 60, 142
Eyedropper tool, 43–44

F

Facebook, 167
Families, typeface, 9, 16
Flaps, 57, 124–125, 140
Flood varnish, 113
FOB (free on board), 165
Foil emboss / stamp, 130–131
Fonts, 9, 40–41
Footers, 98–99
Fractions, 83–84, 196
Freight superfamily, 9–10, 16
French flaps, 57, 124–125, 140
French fold dust jackets, 125–126
Front cover, 54–55
Front matter, 68, 69, 71, 93–94
Fulfillment, 163–164
Full Justify, 30

G

Genesis Framework, 175–176
Gloss lamination, 151
Glossary of terms, 187–194
Glyphs, 11–12
Google Fonts, 8
Google Keyword Tool, 178
Grams per Square Meter (GSM), 197, 198
Graphics, 51–52, 55. See also Photographs and images
Grid system, 75, 76, 77–80
Gusseted hardcover endpaper pockets, 133

H

Hanging quotes, 25
Hardcover books
cover wraps, 82, 109–110
dimensions, 36
endpaper pockets, 133
picture books, 87
spines and bindings, 111, 139–140, 147–149, 197
Head and tail bands, 122
Headers and footers, 98–99
Headlines, 30
Helvetica typeface family, 9
Hierarchy, 6, 40
Hollow square spines, 147
Hook and loop pocket envelopes, 133
Hosting, website, 174–175
Hyphens, 26

I

ICC profiles, 145
Images. See Photographs and images
InDesign
binding, 82
book page layout, 50
color printing, 47, 146–147
duotones, 119
endpapers, 117, 146–147
foil emboss / stamp, 130–131
French fold dust jacket, 126
General tab, 152
grid, 77–80
manuscript, placing in, 58
Marks and Bleeds tab, 153
Output tab, 153
placing manuscript into, 100
planning a book, 34
printing on press, 152–153
soft cover books, 107, 124–125
spot varnish, 128–129
Swatches, 43, 47
tip-on cover stickers, 127
Inks, adding on press, 143
Instagram, 167
Interior pages, 91–101, 146
ISBN, 56–57, 104–105, 158–159, 164
Italic type, 97

J

Journal with elastic band, 132

K

Kerning, 11, 28, 34, 39–40

L

Ladders, 24–25
Lamination, 123, 151
Layout, 4, 6–7, 14, 50–53
Leading, 18, 97

Leaves, 67
Left alignment, 30
Left Justify, 30
Ligatures, 83
Line length, 18
"Look Inside" feature on Amazon, 173, 180

M

MailChimp, 181
Manuscript, 57–58, 100
Marketing, 168–169. See also Selling and
    marketing
Master pages, 14, 50, 52, 53, 89, 96, 97
Matte lamination, 151
Myriad Pro Condensed, 17, 18

N

Notch bound books, 150
Novels, 33, 45, 85, 99

O

Open Type, 10, 39
Open Wire-O, 111, 148, 150
Orphans, 24

P

Package deals, 157–159
Page, defined, 67
Page layout, 6–7, 14, 50–53
Page margins, 28, 48–49, 96
Page numbers, 93–94, 95–96
Pantone Color Bridge, 13, 47, 89, 143, 146
Pantone Library, 47, 143
Pantone Matching System, 46, 47, 118, 119, 133
Paper stock, 38, 41–42, 145–147, 197–198
Paperback books. See Soft cover books
Paragraph styles, 15, 21, 96–97, 98
PDFs, creating to print on press, 152–153
Perfect bound books, 87, 149–150
Photographs and images
    collecting, 59–60
    color in, 59–60
    creating new, 61–62
    credit for, 52
    getting started, 80
    inspiration, finding, 52
    resolution for book printing, 60–63
Photography and art books, 85
Photoshop, 61–62
Picture books, 86–87, 99
Pinterest business pages, 167
Planning a book, 33–65
Pleasing color, 60, 142
PMS (Pantone Matching System), 46, 47, 118,
    119, 133
POD books. See Print-on-demand (POD) books
Pricing, 105–106, 161–162, 173
Printed endpapers, 115–117

Printing on press
    book binding, 139–141
    book printing, 138–139
    color printing, 141–147
    endpapers, 116–117
    hardcover spines and bindings, 147–149
    PDFs, creating, 152–153
    soft cover spines and bindings, 149–151
Print-on-demand (POD) books
    cover wraps, 87
    dimensions, 36–38
    endpapers, 115
    ISBN and barcode, 104
    page margins, 48, 49
    picture books, 86
    printing and binding, 137–138, 140–141
    safe margins, 28
Process color, 45–46, 142, 146, 147
Publisher branding, 159–160
Publisher Record Number, 158, 159
PUR glue, 150

Q

Quotes, 56

R

Recto, 67
Reference books, 89, 99
Repetition, 7
Resolution, 60–63
Resources, 195
Retail pricing, 105–106, 161–162, 173
Rezing up, 61
RGB, 13, 43, 44, 62, 89, 141
Ribbon markers, 123
Right alignment, 31
Rosette, 141, 142
Round spines, 148
Royalties, 158–159

S

Safe margins, 28, 48
Sales message, 55–56
Sans serif typeface, 8, 9, 40, 41
Search Engine Optimization (SEO), 177–179
Selling and marketing
    Amazon, 162–163, 164–165
    branding, 159–160
    distribution, 164–166
    fulfillment, 163–164
    marketing, 168–169
    package deals, 157–159
    pricing strategy, 161–162
    social media, 166–167
    on website, 179–180
Semi-concealed Wire-O, 111, 148–149, 150
Serif typeface, 8, 9, 40, 41
Shrink-wrapped books, 110
Side-sewn books, 140–141

Signatures, 37, 67, 138
Single page layout, 53
Sitebuilders, 171–172
SiteGround, 174
Slip cases, 120
Smyth Sewn books, 37, 140, 141, 147, 149
Social media, 166–167
Soft cover books
    dimensions, 36
    French flaps, 124–125, 140
    picture books, 87
    spines and bindings, 106–107, 111, 140, 149–151
Soft touch lamination, 151
Space between sentences, 22
Spine, 57, 106–110
Spot color, 46, 143, 146
Spot varnish, 113, 128–129
Square spines, 147
Star Print Brokers
    bleeds, 29
    board books, 88
    book dimensions, 38, 85
    book sleeves, 131
    bumper boxes, 121
    color printing, 144, 145
    color scheme, 44
    cover wrap, 87
    delivery and shipping costs, 165
    dust jackets, 113, 125
    endpapers, 87
    ISBN and barcode, 159
    lamination, 151
    minimum orders, 106, 157, 162
    page margins, 49
    paper stock, 38, 41, 42, 197, 198
    photos and images, 59, 60, 61, 62
    printing, 137, 161
    reference books, 89
    safe margins, 29
    slip cases, 120
    social media, 166
    spines and bindings, 137, 147, 149
    website, 174, 176, 179
StudioPress, 176
Style, 5
Subject matter, 5
Subtitle, 55
Superfamilies, typeface, 9–10, 40
Swiss Style Design, 75–76

T

Tail bands, 122
Terms, glossary of, 187–194
Testimonials, 56
Text, 30, 68, 70, 71, 88
Text lines, 80
Text stock, 197
Tight square spines, 147

Time required to design a book, 65
Tints, 43
Tip-on cover stickers, 127
Title, 54–55
Tracking, 19, 28, 34
Twitter, 166, 167, 168
Two-page spreads, 49, 53
Typefaces
    choosing, 39–42
    classifications, 8–9
    contrast, 40
    defined, 9
    families, 9, 16
    non-variable, adjusting, 11
    overused, 23
    size, 17, 19
    superfamilies, 9–10, 40
Typographer's quotes, 22
Typography, 8–12

U

Uncoated paper, 38, 146, 197
United States Postal Service, 131
Unsplash.com, 52, 59

V

Variable Fonts, 10
Vellum tip-in sheets, 126
Verso, 67

W

Websites
    child themes, 176
    color, 177
    domain names, 175
    email list and newsletters, 179–181
    established, 172–173
    hosting, 174–175
    Search Engine Optimization, 177–179
    selling on, 179–180
    signup forms, 181
    sitebuilders, 171–172
    WordPress, 174–177
    White space, 7, 20, 80–81
Widows, 24
Wire-O bindings, 111–112, 148–149, 150
WordPress, 174–177
Words over same words, 27
Words per page, 64

X

X-height, 40

Y

Yoast SEO plugin, 178, 180

Z

Zapf Dingbats, 12

THE LAST PAGE OF A BOOK IS ALWAYS A LEFT-HAND PAGE

198 BOOK DESIGN: SIMPLE & PROFESSIONAL

INDEX (IF CONTINUED) | USE FOOTER OR HEADER | USE PAGE NUMBER
IF BLANK, NO FOOTER, HEADER, OR PAGE NUMBER